Psychotherapy and the Promiscuous Patient

Psychotherapy and the Promiscuous Patient

E. Mark Stern
Editor
Iona College, New Rochelle, New York

Routledge
Taylor & Francis Group
New York London

First published 1992 by The Haworth Press, Inc.

Published 2021 by Routledge
605 Third Avenue, New York, NY 10017
2 Park Square, Milton Park, Abingdon, Oxon OX14 4RN

Routledge is an imprint of the Taylor & Francis Group, an informa business

***Psychotherapy and the Promiscuous Patient* has also been published as *The Psychotherapy Patient*, Volume 8, Numbers 1/2 1992.**

Library of Congress Cataloging-in-Publication Data

Psychotherapy and the promiscuous patient / E. Mark Stern, editor.
p. cm.
"Has also been published as the Psychotherapy patient, volume 8 numbers 1/2, 1992."–T.p. verso.
Includes bibliographical references.
ISBN 1-56024-316-3 (alk. paper).–ISBN 1-56024-317-1 (paper : alk. paper)
1. Promiscuity–Psychological aspects. 2. Promiscuity–Treatment. 3. Psychotherapy. I. Stern, E. Mark, 1929- .
[DNLM: 1. Psychotherapy. 2. Sex Behavior. W1 PS87 v.8 no. 1/2 / WM 420 P975355358]
RC560.P76P86 1992
DNLM/DLC
for Library of Congress **92-49176**
CIP

ISBN 13: 978-1-56024-316-8 (hbk)

Psychotherapy and the Promiscuous Patient

CONTENTS

ABOUT THE EDITOR

E. Mark Stern, EdD, is Graduate Professor in the School of Arts and Sciences, Iona College, New Rochelle, New York. A Diplomate in Clinical Psychology of the American Board of Professional Psychology and a Fellow of the American Psychological Association and the American Psychological Society, Dr. Stern is Past President of the Division of Humanistic Psychology, APA. He is in private practice of psychotherapy with offices in New York City and Dutchess County, New York. Dr. Stern completed his clinical studies at Columbia University (1955) and at the Institute of the National Psychological Association for Psychoanalysis.

More Than a Romp
(A Preface)

Promiscuity signifies more than a random romp. In a relating society, it behooves each person to respect the common interest, not only in the workplace but in the larger context of social relationships. Promiscuity as a defiance of relatedness misses the point of the social order.

Promiscuity, unleashed and relentless in its pursuits, pits the erotic against personal and social controls. Expressions of the promiscuous are woven into the fragility of personal boundaries. Even so, repetitive episodes of sexual and social promiscuity happen when people allow themselves to be deceived into sensory and emotional stagnation.

In the face of apathy, the imagination atrophies. This degeneration of fantasy alienates and provokes compulsive acting-out. Such promiscuous compulsive behavior is antithetical to productive fantasy. Fantasy helps reinforce the boundaries between impulse and action, while the suppression of the imaginal is capable of provoking runaway promiscuous actions.

Promiscuous acting-out prevents fantasy from doing its work. The human romance with intrigue, malediction, and gestures of power unsatisfactorily bond with free-ranging sexual "entitlement." Still, sexual morality, if it be any answer at all, must indeed be worth the sacrifices it demands. The psyche must be taught how to befriend the imaginal, thus leaving the person freer to draw upon the broader repertoire of inner resources.

Good psychotherapy responds to any compulsive behavior by helping individuals make better use of their imaginative potentials.

In responding to the proliferation of promiscuity, responsible psychotherapists help their clientele confront freewheeling sexual activity as one other form of vicarious narcissism. And typical of any unproductive narcissism, promiscuity ultimately fails to address the pain and loneliness of personal existence.

This monograph makes accessible an assemblage of explorations around a theme. Yet even as the lines are drawn, the equivalents of promiscuity must be granted due respect. For even out of the self-abasement of promiscuity, there emerge models which revere respectful non-exclusivity in personal relationships as well as in psychotherapeutic practice.

E. Mark Stern
Editor

Assessment of Promiscuous Behavior

Gordon Baumbacher

SUMMARY. Promiscuous behavior has become increasingly risky. Some patients engage in damaging and dangerous behavior against their best interests and at times against their better judgment. Education alone often fails to curb such behavior when it serves an important role in the individual's psychological organization. This paper will address the various emotional needs that promiscuity may meet, and will briefly address strategies for therapeutic intervention.

With the reemergence of lethal sexually transmitted diseases, clinicians must be concerned by promiscuity in their patients. Education, valuable as it is, alone often fails to curb such behavior. In spite of knowledge, people frequently act against what they know to be in their best interests. This paper will provide a framework for evaluating the motives that override reason, sometimes with tragic consequences.

Promiscuity is a concept with varying meanings. It may be used to describe behavior or to pass judgment on behavior or on the person exhibiting such behavior. In addition, promiscuity has had differing meanings in different times and cultures. Often it has carried implicit or explicit pejorative judgments that have been significantly gender relative. Men and women were not judged by the same standard regarding their sexual conduct. In order to mini-

Gordon Baumbacher, MD, is a graduate of Northwestern University Medical School. He completed his residency training in psychiatry at the University of California in San Francisco when he served as chief resident. He has been on the faculty there since 1976. He is a graduate of the San Francisco Psychoanalytic Institute.

Mailing address: University of California–SF, 401 Parnassus Ave., San Francisco, CA 94143.

mize such relativism and the moral evaluations that are usually unhelpful in clinical fields, I will offer a definition of promiscuity based on behavioral criteria. Promiscuity is sexual behavior with multiple partners which is physically or emotionally damaging to the individual engaging in it (Fluker, 1983).

While behavioral criteria for promiscuity provide a definition, they do not give any account or understanding of the meaning of the behavior to a particular individual. It is important to recognize that behaviors that appear similar may have very different meanings in different people, and, therefore, may be prompted by different motives and represent varying psychological purposes. Thus promiscuity may serve different psychological organizations and needs leading to sexually self-destructive acts with very diverse meanings which, if viewed only as behavior, may appear similar.

Patterns of behavior which are self-destructive generally are prompted by complex motives. While gratification may be present, it is rarely the most important motive since in overall effect self-destructive behavior is ungratifying. Usually such behaviors have pronounced defensive components. They serve a purpose which the individual from the perspective of his or her psychology at a given time or in a given set of circumstances perceives to be the best available way that he or she has to protect self from some threat or damage. Mostly the threat is not external but internal and relates to how the person experiences self and the relationships to others and perceived dangers or vulnerabilities in those situations. Perception and experience of vulnerability are not solely an objective entity but are significantly determined by individual psychological makeup. As a consequence, they will be strongly influenced by past experiences and developmental history.

Psychological organization may be assessed in varying ways, however, a developmental perspective is particularly useful (Settlage, 1980). The path through development requires the emergence and mastery of new capacities and abilities. As new capacities bring the potential for management of more complex functions, they also create new perceptions including new views of self and of the world which of necessity are accompanied by new and unique anxieties.

Although developmental events do not have a simple, direct

correlation with adult difficulties, stages of developmental organization provide a useful paradigm for adult experience and assessment of disorders. Vulnerabilities and fears are shaped in the mold of developmental anxieties since these represent the models of emotional danger with which people have had experience. In the following, promiscuity will be discussed from this developmental perspective. As a behavior it will have different meanings and motivations depending upon the level of psychological organization of the person utilizing it. In this sense promiscuity itself is not the basic problem but a symptom of a problem which the individual attempts to manage by driven and destructive sexual behavior. Promiscuity also can occur in other types of disorders which are beyond the scope of this paper. For example, hypersexual behavior may be a part of bipolar affective disorders, some types of organic brain syndrome, and substance abuse. These should be considered in a differential diagnosis.

While individual experiences of development are infinitely varied and each person's life story is different, there are common themes that bridge individual differences. These similarities result from the sequential unfolding of developmental milestones marked by the emergence of new capacities. As these capacities make possible new abilities, they simultaneously carry the liability of generating new vulnerabilities and, therefore, anxieties based upon new fears. As these new abilities and anxieties are exercised and experienced in the child's life, they both will be shaped and modulated by innate characteristics of temperament and by environmental influences (Engel, 1962).

The first major developmental task involves acquiring a relatively stable sense of self as a separate individual in the world. Generally this occurs over the first 2 to 3 years of life and has several substages. Achievement of the stable capacity to view oneself as separate is of major importance for future development and ultimately for adult functioning. Upon it is based the ability to reality test, that is, to distinguish internal stimuli from external stimuli, to tolerate being alone, to internally regulate self esteem and to control impulsivity. Failure to acquire some or all of these functions has important consequences regarding promiscuous behavior.

At birth infants do not have the psychological abilities or mental organization to experience themselves as separate entities with an existence and boundaries distinct from the rest of the world and those who care for them. While infants cannot describe their experiences, much objective data on development from birth onward is now available. No evidence suggests that initially infants have an ability to construct a stable internal, mental world in which they perceive themselves to exist separately from environment and caregivers. Much evidence suggests that they do not (Spitz, 1965). As a consequence, they do not comprehend that their wishes are separate from effects, or that others are different people who may have independent motives. There is not the ability to hold in memory images of people or objects that are not present, and modulation of feeling states is very dependent upon the environment and parenting figures (Fraiberg, 1969).

From infancy through about the first 2 years of life, there is increasing ability first to recognize specific people who are important in the child's life and then to begin to integrate into a multidimensional composite the different aspects of those people along with the child's associated feelings (Mahler, 1965). As affect is a major organizer of memory, during this period the child has part memories of important people such as parents and caregivers in which a set of memories is united by an associated affect. In this period different feeling states evoke linked memories that capture a part of the person but which are not yet integrated with other feeling states and associated memories. Thus the good and gratifying mother is not comprehended simultaneously as the same person who at other times frustrates. Prior to integration these fragmented object representations give rise to a developmentally normal and usually transient phase of splitting. There is no whole representation of others with multifaceted characteristics, some of which simultaneously evoke likes and dislikes or love and hatred that can be sustained in the presence of strong feelings or in the absence of the actual person.

The capacity to integrate these part representations into a composite image that can be both loved and hated at the same time and that can be remembered intact even when the person whom the image represents is not present marks a major developmental milestone. It is termed object constancy and is heralded by the onset of a capacity for ambivalence. Ambivalence is manifested by this ability to experience simultaneously for the same person opposite affects such as love and anger or hate.

Prior to the onset of object constancy the infant is extremely dependent upon external figures to maintain his or her inner world of mental representations. Without constant support, the representations in the child's mental world begin to disintegrate, and without them their self-regulatory functions are lost as well. Thus the capacity to comfort self when alone is lost, as is any capacity internally to modulate anxiety, maintain self-esteem, control impulses, or accurately distinguish between stimuli of external and internal origin. To be alone for any length of time becomes intolerable. Mahler (1975) has described the constant need for children struggling with separation issues to frequently touch base with the mother, a process she has termed as "refueling."

Once the capacity for relatively stable representations has been developed at between 2 and 3 years of age, children have a much greater potential for internal self-regulation and for an understanding of themselves as separate beings in the world. This new capacity for differentiation between self and others also creates a new anxiety. Formerly without self-and-other differentiation the child had been able to maintain fantasies of omnipotence. The lack of a clear distinction between self and parent permitted the child to imagine that the adults' power was also the child's own. Idealized, grandiose parent figures could merge into grandiose images of self. In addition without a sense of self as separate, parental response to the child's needs were experienced as caused by his or her wishes rather than by the parent as an independent agent responding to the child's needs. With the realization of the self as a separate entity in the world, that comforting feeling of omnipotence is lost and with its demise come the fear and anxiety of recognizing oneself to be small, separate, and relatively helpless in the world.

The advent of object constancy with the potential for greater real control and perceptual clarity now entails new problems. The child must experience and manage the injury of losing the very comforting sense of omnipotence, and without it is confronted with the realization of his or her real helplessness in the world, particularly in regard to powerful adult figures.

Much of what has been termed the "terrible twos" results from the child's attempts to deal with this sense of helplessness and loss of control (White, 1975). Self and object differentiation, however, makes possible the use of aggression expressed as sadism in an attempt to regain lost control. By definition, sadism is the experience of pleasure in inflicting pain or suffering upon another. This, of course, requires the capacity to experience another as a separate entity. At this point children use the newfound sadism in an attempt to regain a sense of mastery. Children of this age often react with anger when their desire or will is thwarted. Frustrated two-year-olds frequently hit, punch, pinch, and twist when they do not get their way. In effect, the child says that if you frustrate me, I will hurt you and then you will do what I want.

Usually the injury resulting from the loss of omnipotent fantasies is mastered in time. The child is able to accept that he or she, like everyone, must tolerate limits and limitations. In some instances, however, circumstances may compromise this mastery. Factors that make helplessness more threatening will increase difficulty in managing the anxiety of this phase. For instance, increased innate aggressiveness may have such an effect, as may parental responses which needlessly accentuate the child's inevitable sense of powerlessness. Excessively controlling caregivers, by depriving the child of reasonable feelings of power and control, amplify the painful experiences of helplessness. Similarly, caregivers who are unresponsive during this phase also increase the child's sense of ineffectiveness. If experiencing helplessness has been intolerably painful, it cannot be processed but instead remains a threat against which protection must be constantly maintained. Then an ongoing vigil is required to retain control and prevent its usurpation by others.

When control is no longer a major preoccupation, the developing child is faced with other affectively charged issues. Increased cognitive capacities permit the child to be more aware of others and to make comparisons. Thus around the age of three both little boys and little girls become aware of and preoccupied with the differences between the sexes. Each, through the cognitive and psychological organization that he or she has at the time, attempts to make sense of what they observe. Each also is interested in showing off his or her abilities or prowess. Thus little boys begin to struggle with the awareness that women have babies and men do not (Jacobson, 1950). Little boys of this age regularly have pregnancy fantasies and are hesitant to accept that they can never grow and birth babies. The power to create life is awesome, and to a child it is particularly so. For this reason as well as the mother's usual nurturing role in regard to the very young, mothers and women are experienced as particularly powerful and enviable figures. The recognition for little boys that they will never be able to perform in this powerful way is extremely deflating. They may protect against it by devaluing feminine attributes.

As boys and girls notice sex roles and body differences, their interactions are for a while partly shaped by these observations. Little boys become phallic in behavior, they relate through being intrusive and penetrating. For example, they poke constantly at others and they play preferentially with phallic toys such as sticks and guns. Their pattern of relating during this stage is intrusive.

This phallic preoccupation exhibited by little boys leads to a second injury to their self-esteem. Not only must they accept that in spite of their wishes they will not be able to have babies and to give life, but, in addition, they are disappointed in their fantasies of being phallically powerful. During this period mothers remain of major importance to both boys and girls. As intrusive behavior is a principle mode of interaction, both wish to be able to phallically possess those whom they love (Baumbacher & Amini, 1981). Boys are further disappointed by their relative phallic inadequacy in regard to their mothers. In a different way little boys are again confronted by the limitations of reality in the face of their wishes.

Little girls also are faced with disappointment of their phallic wishes (Kestenberg, 1968). For them the injury is the recognition that they will not be able to possess their mothers in this mode. They are less concerned with phallic potential itself, than with the worry of being inadequate in regard to their desire (as have all children) to be capable of attaining the person whom they love.

For both boys and girls these disappointments are experienced as injuries to their self-esteem. If the injury is manageable, the child copes with the disappointment, accepts it, and goes on to other tasks. When the disappointment becomes too great the child is unable to accept it and remains on some level preoccupied with trying to rectify an impossible situation. In such an instance the patterns and anxieties of this period are likely to shape future experience and relationships.

Children are more likely to have difficulty mastering the phallic-stage disappointment if they are already insecure in their self-esteem. For instance, children who begin this phase with existing depression or who doubt the security of their maternal attachment will be more vulnerable to further disappointments, particularly those that generate worry regarding parental love. For example, mothers who are themselves depressed and devalue themselves as women create added difficulties for their daughters. Little girls much more easily accept phallic disappointment if they see their mothers as confident women with whom they can identify.

After the phallic phase, patterns of relationship have a different quality. Through the phallic phase children's object relationships are organized principally in a diadic mode of interaction. That is, their attention is directed toward one person at a time. Others may be seen as obstacles to their goals, but not yet as participants in a more complex interchange. After the phallic phase, however, with the push of development and the capacity for less self-referential thought, interpersonal themes become triadic. Children by the age of four to six begin to understand that others may have motives that conflict with their own. As a consequence, they become concerned with competition from others, particularly in regard to a loved parent. Children immersed in this phase, the oedipal phase, seem compelled to create in their minds competition from a third person for the object of their love. Since children love both of their parents, they simultaneously love each parent and feel rivalry with each parent for the other. From such a situation there is no solution. To imagine defeating one parent for the love of the other is simultaneously to lose one who also is loved and win one who is a rival as well. Not surprisingly, children during the oedipal phase become quite anxious and normally develop transient anxiety symptoms such as phobias and night fears.

Since no solution is possible, attempted resolutions are doomed to failure for the child or for the adult who remains preoccupied with oedipal issues. The result is repetitive unsuccessful patterns of behavior. Such patterns are the heart of neuroses which are in essence an inability to give up on a riddle that has no answer. Children, however, are unable to give up these issues. To do so requires the capacity to let go of parents as primary figures of love, which cannot be done until adolescence.

Much of the process of adolescence involves the relinquishing of parents as primary figures of attachment (Blos, 1962). Children are unable psychologically to let go of parents because prior to adolescence parents are essential for survival and development. Preadolescents' need for parental figures is well attested by their reaction to inadequate or absent parents. In such situations children will go to great lengths to exonerate their parents of shortcomings even to the point of blaming themselves for outright abuse. Only when youngsters, through maturation and learning, have acquired the necessary ego functions and capacities can parents who previously supplied those not-yet-developed functions be relinquished. During adolescence the developmental process adds the necessary abilities for independent functioning in the world. Adolescence then provides the possibility of the only real solution to oedipal strivings–relinquishing the goal itself.

The successful path through adolescence is prepared during latency which spans the 6 to 7 years onward from the oedipal period. Relationships during latency retain to a significant extent an oedipal (triadic) configuration. They are less overt because the latency-age child reduces their apparent intensity through repression. The usefulness of repression as a defense is greatly increased by the organization of superego functions at the end of the oedipal period. Guilt, the marker of superego formation, prompts repression and derives its force from the motives and anxieties of the oedipal struggle. As noted earlier, the oedipal struggle when experienced unameliorated is highly anxiety provoking. The first escape from the dilemma of aggression toward an also-loved parent is attempted by projecting that motive onto the parent. Thus children during this period imagine parents to be angry with them whether or not they actually are. However, to live with a loved caretaker who is experienced as hostile is only a slight improvement. Temporary solutions to the resulting uncomfortable state account for many of the anxiety symptoms of the age, such as phobias in which the projected aggression is displaced to a neutral object.

A more adaptive alternative involves the establishment of the rudiments of superego functioning (Loewald, 1980). The projected aggression is reinternalized as prohibitions on fantasies and impulses involving oedipal themes. Instead of being aware of aggressive and incestuous wishes the child begins to feel anxious if those thoughts start to enter awareness and attempts to exclude them from conscious representation. The aggression initially involved in oedipal themes has been projected, possibly displaced, and then reinternalized as internal prohibitions on certain kinds of fantasies and wishes. In development this process represents one of the clearest examples of projective identification. With repression of oedipal themes the child is freer to focus attention on non-need-bound tasks and is ready to enter latency.

With the completion of adolescence development does not cease. Data support the view that new themes emerge in adulthood and that these new phenomena take place in the context of established character. Character formation is initiated with the completion of adolescence and is solidified during early adult phases. Character represents the stable pattern or pattern of instability by which the person mediates and compromises between internal needs and demands of the external world. In any given individual it represents a condensation of abilities, liabilities, and desires and fears resulting from developmental life experiences. The formation of character gives predictability to behavior including patterns for problem solving and managing anxiety.

Promiscuous behavior, then, will be compatible with the character organization of the individual in whom it takes place. In all instances it will serve multiple needs, including important defensive functions. The following will describe the meaning and purpose of promiscuity in the various character organizations assessed from a developmental perspective. The various categories discussed will be illustrated with brief clinical examples. As well as these more general meanings, behavior has meaning specific to the individual which will be based upon the specific content of past experiences. These personal meanings are important in the selection of specific behaviors for defensive purposes.

The first large category of disorders involves individuals who as adults have failed to achieve self and other (object) differentiation. They are unable to maintain a stable distinction between representations of themselves and representations of other people. This failure is accompanied by an inability, particularly under stress or in situations that generate strong feelings, to hold an integrated view of self and others that simultaneously permits an awareness of multifaceted characteristics. Without this capacity stable memories and images which are necessary for internal regulation of self-esteem and for tolerance of being alone are not available. As a consequence, these individuals are highly vulnerable to unmanageable depression and intense anxiety when by themselves; and they become highly dependent upon others to provide those functions which they lack but which protect against severe pain.

The resultant hunger for contact with others in patients with this type of ego deficit can promote highly promiscuous behavior. Sex becomes a vehicle for establishing at least transient contact with someone–anyone–when vital mental representations begin to crumble. The specific person is relatively unimportant as long as he or she can meet the narcissistic needs that help the patient to stabilize the internal world and regulation of mood, which then lessens otherwise intolerable anxiety or depression. In this regard, troubled adolescents are particularly vulnerable to using sexual activity in an attempt to regulate self-esteem and affect (Giovacchini, 1986). In treatment these individuals need to be helped to develop more adaptive ways to manage their feelings.

A young woman with intermittent, highly promiscuous behavior illustrated this condition well. She had grown up in a chaotic family with an absent father and an alcoholic, psychotic mother. Because of the inconsistent, explosive reactions of her mother when she was little, she had no opportunity to develop an internal world of stable representations. Instead, people existed for her as transient part objects tied both to her mood and her immediate interactions with them. As a result, she was very vulnerable to others and very vulnerable to being without them. Stress threatened her fragile ego functions, which in turn generated further anxiety. The more anxious she became, the less she could rely upon her frail capacities to regulate her mood and judgment. At such times she became desperate to make contact with anyone, lest her anxiety increase out of control as she feared it would. Frequently, in her desperation, she used sex to obtain that contact.

In such a situation promiscuity, even with all of its inherent risks, is a protection against such a powerful fear that it cannot be addressed successfully without alleviating the intensity of the anxiety that prompts it. In this patient treatment was directed toward assisting her in maintaining her vulnerable ego functions. Of particular importance was helping her to keep intact mental representations of herself and others without confusing or merging them.

In individuals in whom object constancy has been established, a different set of anxieties may lead to promiscuous behavior. Initially, realization of self as separate leads to anxiety regarding awareness of helplessness and loss of fantasies of omnipotence. If those feelings have remained intolerable, sex may be used as a way to regain a sense of control. In such instances sadism or at least sadistic fantasies will be a part of the meaning of sexual behavior. This dynamic is exemplified by the following case. A woman in her mid-thirties had a history of rapidly becoming sexually involved with men whom she found superficially interesting but who usually treated her poorly. Often these men "like to party," a trait that she found appealing. She would drink with them and then later regret having gone to bed with them. The relationships mostly were brief and stormy. Her family background was characterized by an ineffective mother and an alcoholic, seductive, unreliable father. The mother who had been reasonably attentive during the patient's infancy had become threatened by her developing push for autonomy as a child. The mother reacted with a combination of excessive control and rejection. The father had been intermittently, superficially interested in the patient but always his interest soon turned into self-interest. These repeated disappointments had increased her feelings of helplessness.

The patient's seemingly masochistic sexual behavior was interwoven with controlling and sadistic themes. Her parents' approach to her had fostered extreme feelings of helplessness and anger with which she also had felt powerless. The reactions were increased by identification with her mother's inadequacy and were covertly directed against the seductive and frustrating father. As a result, she was both enraged with and contemptuous of men. Her attitudes toward men were expressed secretly through her sexual behavior. While superficially seeming to admire men she could feel in control of them through sex and feel disdain for them in their need of her.

She would not give up the promiscuous behavior even though she consciously wanted to do so until in treatment she felt mastery over her fear of intolerable helplessness.

A second psychological organization arising from diadic-level issues in which promiscuity may be a defense involves phallic phase themes. Here repeated sexual conquest serves as a temporary reassurance against feared inadequacy and ultimately against the depression of feeling incapable of obtaining the love of the longed-for mother. Each seduction brings a temporary but hollow relief from anxiety which soon returns. It is, after all, always the wrong woman. The one who is secretly longed for, the disappointing mother, remains forever unattainable.

A man in his early 30s entered treatment with mild depression and the complaint that he was unable to find the right woman with whom to sustain a relationship. He had had numerous infatuations, but after an intense romance found that he lost interest, feeling that the woman somehow was not right. In the course of the treatment it became clear that he clung to a fantasy that if he tried hard enough he would be able to obtain his mother's consistent affection. She had been a capricious, single woman who frequently had left him to involve herself with various men. As a child he had felt himself to be inadequate to obtain her interest and as an adult endlessly attempted to overcome his past disappointment. He could be in love with a woman when she, like his mother, was elusive. However, as soon as he won her affection he lost interest. The woman of his fantasies could never be obtained. The patient was able to give up this unsuccessful pattern only after he had reexperienced and reworked in the treatment the very painful feelings of rejection and imagined inadequacy.

Issues that are organized at a triadic level also may prompt promiscuous behavior. In those instances the person has been unable to relinquish the hope and quest for a solution to mutually exclusive goals which are simultaneously sought during the oedipal phase. Victory on the one hand immediately and inevitably engenders defeat on the other hand. For multiple reasons, including vulnerabilities incurred earlier or actual events or interactional patterns that amplify existing anxieties, the parental figures embodied in images and memories from this phase may be difficult to release as normally occurs during adolescence. This attachment remains a source of ongoing difficulty. It should be noted that promiscuity is only one of many maladaptive solutions to oedipal issues. When it does occur, as in other disorders, it serves multiple purposes in psychological organization. For instance, it can maladaptively provide the enactment of a fantasied solution by seeming to offer a victory which simultaneously is punished with defeat and suffering.

A young woman sought treatment with a complaint that she felt used in repeated relationships with men who were already involved with someone else. It soon became apparent that she was only interested in men who already had established relationships. Although she consciously felt used, her interest in these men lasted only as long as the other women were more successful rivals. If the men began to move toward her as the primary and exclusive relationship, she quickly lost interest in them and became anxious and depressed. These men fit into her fantasy of supplementing her mother in her father's affection. The fantasy had been both stimulated and made frightening by her father's covert seductiveness and overt denigration of the mother, who had been incapacitated following a serious accident. In the apparent victory she simultaneously imagined further injury to her mother whom she unconsciously felt she had already injured through her actual closeness with her father. Although she had consciously somewhat adopted his denigrating attitude toward the mother, she actually had great affection for her and was very worried that she had and would harm her. In the behavior patterns of her present life she retold her story, both the imagined criminal victory and the punishment. She punished herself not only with her anxiety and depression but also through her chronically unsuccessful patterns in which she overall achieved only defeat of herself. In treatment a pivotal aspect of altering these patterns involved her recognition of her deep love for her mother and her fright at recognizing it. It frightened her because she also felt strongly competitive with her. Once she recognized all the parts of this struggle and was less threatened by the feelings connected with them, she was able to tolerate the pain of giving up on the sad and unchangeable situation that had been her family.

Promiscuity may have many different forms as well as causes. In general, the promiscuity resulting from earlier issues with concomitant greater psychological damage has a more primitive cast in which less capacity to relate to people as distinct individuals is revealed (Kernberg, 1974). In those whose difficulties spring from failure to maintain whole, stable representations of self and other, sexual behavior often has a driven, desperate quality. Partners are more readily substituted with less capacity for any sustained attachment. They are experienced more as an extension of need rather than as independent individuals. Feelings are dependent on the moment and such patients have a greater tendency to externalize their problems and less capacity to reflect upon their action. Similarly, the capacity for good reality testing and judgment is likely to be reduced, especially when it conflicts with the demands of emotional needs. Thus these patients are less able to protect themselves and run greater emotional and physical risks.

As patients possess more integrated psychological organization, they are likely to exhibit more of a capacity for self-observation and self-evaluation. Sexual behavior, even if promiscuous, is less blatantly driven, carried out in a more socially appropriate manner, and more likely to induce worry and guilt. These patients usually are able to take better care of themselves and to be less overtly self-destructive. In their relationship, they are capable of a genuine appreciation of the other person.

Committed relationships in which love is sustained require a significant degree of health. Generally it requires the ability to enter relationship in which the other person is perceived to be an individual in his or her own right rather than an extension of needs and self-referential attitudes. In addition, it requires sufficient freedom from primary attachments to parental figures to permit entering new relationships without recasting them as repetitious of or reactions against the old ones.

Where problems with sustained intimacy arise, promiscuity can represent one method by which the person attempts to effect a solution to the fundamental difficulty. Like any symptom it is both maladaptive and the best adaptation the person can make at the time. Patients with this problem are helped most if the therapist undertakes an assessment that provides an understanding of patients' character organization and the role this behavior plays in meeting their needs and fears.

REFERENCES

Baumbacher, G., & Amini, F. (1981). The hysterical personality disorder. *International Journal of Psychoanalytic Psychotherapy, 8*, 501-532.

Blos, P. (1962). *On adolescence*. New York: The Free Press.

Engel, G. (1962). *Psychological development in health and disease*. Philadelphia: Saunders.

Fluker, J. (1983). The perils of promiscuity. *Journal of Psychosomatic Research, 27*(2), 153-156.

Fraiberg, S. (1969). Libidinal object constancy and mental representation. *The Psychoanalytic Study of the Child, 24*, 9-47.

Giovacchini, P. (1986). Promiscuity in adolescents and young adults. *Medical Aspects of Human Sexuality*, 24-31.

Jacobson, E. (1950). Development of the wish for a child in boys. *The Psychoanalytic study of the Child, 5*, 139-152.

Kernberg, O. (1968). Barriers to falling and remaining in love. *Journal of the American Psychoanalytic Association, 22*, 486-511.

Kestenberg, J. (1968). Outside and inside, male and female. *Journal of the American Psychoanalytic Association, 16*, 457-520.

Loewald, H. (1980). The warning of the Oedipus complex. *Papers on psychoanalysis* (pp. 384-404). New Haven: Yale University Press.

Mahler, M. (1965). On the significance of the normal separation-individuation phase. In M. Schur (Ed.), *Drives, affects, behaviors* (Vol. 2, pp. 161-169). New York: International Universities Press.

Mahler, M., Pine, F., & Bergman, A. (1975). *The psychological birth of the human infant*. New York: Basic Books.

Settlage, C. (1980). Psychoanalytic developmental thinking in current and historic perspective. *Psychoanalysis and Contemporary Thought, 3*(2), 139-170.

Spitz, R. (1965). *The first year of life*. New York: International Universities Press.

White, B. (1975). *The first three years of life*. New York: Avon Books.

Adult Promiscuity Following Childhood Sexual Abuse: An Introduction

Robert J. Timms
Patrick Connors

SUMMARY. Sexual abuse happens to approximately one in three females and one in five males before age eighteen. This abuse produces many behavioral, emotional, and physical problems in adult life. One such consequence is adult sexual promiscuity. Anxiety which arises over childhood abuse may be dealt with by compulsive or addictive behaviors. Repressed or forgotten abuse may manifest itself in adult life symptomatically by out-of-control behaviors which are abusive of self and/or others. Such compulsive behaviors reflect an attempt to gain mastery over the original abuse and the abuser. Keeping promiscuous behavior secret reinforces the original abuse pattern and leads to guilt, shame, and isolation. Countertransference issues facing the therapist are discussed. Four case histories show examples of male and female promiscuity following childhood abuse.

Robert J. Timms earned his PhD in clinical psychology from Georgia State University in 1971. Co-founder of the Atlanta Center for Integrative Therapy, he specializes in working with men and women who were physically and sexually abused in childhood. He is on the adjunct faculty of Oglethorpe University, 20 Executive Park West, Suite 2025, Atlanta, GA 30329.

Patrick Connors holds a BS from The Defiance College. Also a co-founder of the Atlanta Center for Integrative Therapy, he is involved in treatment, education, and research in the area of sexual and physical abuse. He is also a certified massage therapist with strong interest in physical as well as emotional consequences of abuse. The authors have written a book entitled *Embodying Healing: Integrating Bodywork and Psychotherapy in Recovery from Chilhood Abuse*, by Safer Society Press, Orwell, VT (in press).

Sexual abuse in childhood casts long and dark shadows over adult life. Several recent publications describe the long-term consequences in adulthood resulting from such abuse (Everstine & Everstine, 1989; Gannon, 1989). Current clinical experience shows as many as 80 percent of hospitalized substance-abuse patients have a history of childhood sexual abuse. Similar findings are reported for patients with eating disorders. We now propose that sexual promiscuity in adult life is another possible consequence of childhood sexual abuse.

Childhood sexual abuse of females is well documented and discussed in professional literature (Russell, 1986). Currently, discussion of sexual abuse of young males is also entering the professional literature (Hunter, 1990; Timms & Connors, 1990). With increased awareness of abuse, and with broader definitions of abuse, it is now estimated that about one in three females are sexually abused before the age of 18, and about one in five males are so abused. It is important to note that there is no direct correlation between the severity of the abuse and the effects in adult life. For example, simple fondling of a child by an adult may cause severe problems when that child reaches maturity which can last well into the adult years. For adult survivors of childhood sexual abuse, there are three possible reactions in the sexual domain. One is a shutting down of awareness and expression of sexual feeling; a second is the developing of normal sexual responsiveness and expression; and a third is becoming sexually promiscuous. The latter, in our opinion, is due to blurring of sexual boundaries as a result of the abusive history.

Adult consequences of childhood abuse frequently include anxiety, depression, dissociative disorders, health issues, hypertension in males, lowered self-esteem, eating disorders, sexual dysfunction, power and control issues, addictive behaviors, and compulsive behaviors including sexual promiscuity.

It is important to see sexual promiscuity as an example of compulsive behavior. Much compulsive behavior is regarded as an attempt to control anxiety and to repress powerful emotions from conscious awareness. By looking at promiscuity as a consequence of childhood sexual abuse, new insights into the promiscuous patient are obtained which allow for new and alternative therapeutic interventions.

One of the most important insights depends on whether the childhood abuse is remembered or repressed. When a person is amnestic about childhood abuse (in our experience, about 25 percent are), the therapist must work with the unconscious presentation of memories, through dreams (particularly traumatic nightmares), emotional and physical symptoms, and specific behaviors such as promiscuity. We have described (Timms & Connors, 1990) ways for the therapist to recognize unconscious presentation of childhood abuse material and thus help the client recover memory of the event. One such disguised presentation involves hypersexuality, often in a promiscuous form. This may frequently be coupled with another compulsive behavior pattern such as alcohol, drug, or food abuse. Clinical data coming from alcohol and drug inpatient treatment programs support this observation. More and more clients from such programs are being referred for treatment of "addictive" sexual behavior. Without entering the argument as to whether or not promiscuity represents addictive behavior, we do recognize it as out-of-control behavior, related to a powerful internal drive which is a manifestation of intense anxiety.

Little of this hypersexuality leads to personal and/or sexual gratification. It is not uncommon for such a person to report that immediately after physical orgasm she or he felt dissatisfied and started feeling shame and guilt. Since the sexual activity did not dissipate the anxiety, the problem is then compounded with the feelings of guilt and shame. In our opinion the promiscuous behavior is an unconscious attempt to control the emotions associated with the original sexual abuse and thus, symbolically, to achieve mastery over the abuser. This sets up for the patient an impossible situation. Instead of mastering the abuse, what typically happens instead is that the patient engages in behaviors which lower her or his self-esteem. The person feels guilty because of failing again to reach what is an impossible goal: mastery of the abuser. Rather than feeling closer and more intimate with the partner, the client instead feels more distant, and also angry or frightened, and wants to get away. The additional guilt and shame add to the problem and lead to a downward spiral. This cycle reinforces negative aspects of sexuality and recreates the emotions of the original abuse, thus deepening the trauma, rather than leading to healing.

Further, since this all is happening at an unconscious level, the patient becomes more confused and uncertain about what is happening. One may feel worthless, even despairing. Suicidal thoughts or fantasies may occur after promiscuous sexual behavior. Other self-abusive behavior often occurs, such as overeating or excessive drinking.

Typically, the promiscuous person does not talk with anyone about his or her sexual experiences. This keeping secret of sexual activity recreates an aspect of the original abuse, which also was kept secret. Just as telling the original secret started the healing process, so telling of current sexual promiscuity to a therapist or to a sex-addicts-anonymous group, will initiate recovery from promiscuous behavior.

Some promiscuous patients carry compulsivity to a higher level by keeping a detailed journal or diary of their sexual exploits. This is invariably a sign of deep personality disturbance and a poor prognostic indicator. The behaviors written down are thus reinforced and the secret becomes more entrenched. The behavior is similar, in this way, to that of some pedophiles who keep detailed notes and records of their victims. The writing is an added layer of compulsivity and secretiveness. It shuts out other, more healthy contacts, thus insulating the promiscuous patient even more in her or his pathology. At an unconscious level, the writing is a confession of the person's inward recognition that the sexual behavior is a problem.

Because of the isolation, guilt, and shame, it can be very difficult for the therapist to reach the patient emotionally and to develop a working alliance. It is important for the therapist to be aware of her or his own issues in this area, and to avoid a judgmental or a punitive stance. In addition, the therapist must avoid undue interest in the details of the reported sexual behavior. Once a promiscuous patient starts talking in therapy about the sexual behavior, he or she may want to give intimate details to see if the therapist is interested or becomes aroused. Working with promiscuous clients will test countertransference issues, particularly around judgment and voyeurism.

Many therapists have been unwilling to recognize males as victims, either in the past (in childhood abuse) or in the present (in revictimization scenarios). Although this situation is changing, one area of countertransference to watch for is a gender-based bias, evaluating males and females differently, both in the areas of promiscuous behavior and of childhood abuse.

The following examples from clinical practice will illustrate various effects of childhood sexual abuse on adult sexual behavior. (All names and identifying information have been changed.) The first shows an example of unconscious influence of childhood abuse. Alan, a 34-year-old dentist, came for treatment after discharge from an inpatient drug rehabilitation program for impaired health professionals. Though treated for a major cocaine addiction, he had also strongly abused alcohol for years. Now drug free, he felt ready to enter intensive personal psychotherapy to deal with some issues he said he had never mentioned in his drug rehabilitation program. Though he was "happily married" and the father of a 14-month-old child, Alan reported that he was sexually promiscuous in a compulsive manner. Whenever he was out driving alone and would pass an adult book store or movie theater, he would go in, seek out the oldest black male in the place (who must be older than Alan), perform fellatio on him, then leave. This behavior would be repeated up to 5 or 6 days a week, and once as often as five times in one day. Alan reported deriving no sexual pleasure from the act (he did not masturbate during the act, nor did he have sexual fantasies during or afterwards). He did not see himself as homosexual, and felt that he did enjoy sexual contact with his wife–though such contact was sporadic and limited. Immediately after each compulsive act, he would report feeling "a rush of energy," which would quickly diminish; then he would start to feel guilty and depressed until the next occurrence. When initially questioned, he did not report any childhood sexual molestation, though he did report being sexually active with both male and female peers during adolescence. He continued to say, though, that he thought there was something he could not remember. Finally, under hypnosis, he recalled an experience as a child of about ten. Visiting relatives at a beach, he had been on his way alone to a movie, when he was accosted by a drunken older black man, who forced Alan to perform fellatio. Alan was very troubled by the experience but never told anyone about it. Very shortly after this attack Alan first started drinking. This eventually led to alcohol abuse, and later led to drug abuse. He forgot about the attack and had never mentioned it to any one until the memory was recalled in therapy. As he saw the connection between his current adult behavior and his childhood abuse, he was able to express directly the strong fears and reactions he had not allowed himself to experience as a child. As these fears and angers were expressed, his depression and anxiety decreased and his promiscuous behaviors stopped. He was able to achieve greater intimacy with his wife. Today he reports being drug and alcohol free for 8 years, and has been able to refrain from his compulsive sexual promiscuity.

Of course, not all childhood abuse is forgotten in adult life. Still, its effect can be profound. Jill, a young woman about 26 years old, entered therapy because she was unhappy and unable to sustain relationships. The initial interview found that she was quite promiscuous in her life, always having sex with a man on her first date with him. Sexual intimacies increased after the first date, usually with Jill being the initiator. She would continue being more and more sexually active with the man until he would stop seeing her. This rejection would lead her onto further dates with other men, constantly seeking love and approval. As therapy progressed, Jill revealed that her father had initiated sex with her when she was 12, and had continued until his sudden death when she was 17. She saw sexual contact with men as an attempt to secure the love and approval she had so desperately wanted from her father. Her constant sexual activity was an attempt to prove to herself that there was nothing wrong with her and that she was lovable. Of course, her constant neediness and approval seeking drove every man away. This intense sexualizing of relationships, as mentioned above, is a basis of sexual compulsivity in adult life, and when combined with lowered self-esteem results in extremely damaging relationships. Therapy with this young woman centered on ego development and toward her seeing the father's behavior as a manifestation of his own needs, not as an interest in or love for her. This working through required some period of grief and loss, but resulted in an increased sense of self-worth and a much improved sense of personal responsibility in selecting partners for sexual and emotional intimacy. At last report, she was married and the mother of two children. She felt "secure and lovable."

As the authors have pointed out (Timms & Connors, 1990), early sexual experiences of young males with older females are frequently not considered abusive in our culture. By applying the same standards to male sexuality as to females, however, the following example will be seen as abusive.

At the age of 13, Ramon was left alone by his parents in their apartment with a 21-year-old maid while the parents went away for a week. During that time, the maid introduced the young man to intercourse, and had sex with him many times, even though Ramon felt both anxious and frightened. Being from a very devout Roman Catholic family, he went to confession twice that week. Though obviously feeling extremely guilty, he never told his family. Later, his mother fired the maid, accusing her of having been sexual with the father. This history was obtained from Ramon when he entered therapy at the age of 33. He was, by that time, an ordained priest, currently in graduate school pursuing a doctorate in philosophy. Ramon was also pursuing almost every female in sight, preferring older women whom he met while in his clerical role. By the time he entered therapy, having been sent by his confessor, he was dating three to five different women a week, and having sex with most of them. With none of them had he developed a true emotionally intimate relationship. Though he could see a connection with his childhood sexual experience (which he did not call abuse) he felt unable to stop his behavior. As his therapy progressed, however, he became clear that the incident at age 13 was abuse. He was then able to see how he, in turn, had been using and abusing the women with whom he had contact. He was finally able to realize that these women were as much under his charge as he had been under the charge of the maid in his thirteenth year. With this insight, his sexual promiscuity stopped. Therapy terminated when he completed his doctorate. At that time, he was again celibate, but was unsure whether he would continue in the priesthood. Follow up data, unfortunately, is not available.

Finally, there is the case of Jerry, a psychiatrist. He came to treatment in his early 40s, with his wife. They presented with marital problems, at first poorly defined. It soon became obvious that Jerry had a severe drinking problem. As treatment continued, it became clear that Jerry and his wife had an "open marriage," and that he was becoming jealous of her contact with another man, with whom Jerry thought she was developing a primary relationship. At this point, the case turned very complex and eventually very messy. His wife accused Jerry of having sex with some of his clients, which he at first denied. He accused her of being "uptight" about sexuality because she had been raped by her father, a charge which she at first denied, but later admitted was true. He presented, in turn, a complex history in which he had been repeatedly physically abused, in a very severe manner, by his father. Eventually, it turned out that this abuse included sexual humiliation, with Jerry as a young boy (about 8 to 10 years old) being forced to watch the father have sex with the mother, and with Jerry being forced to participate.

Although the father died in a car wreck when Jerry was about 10 years of age, Jerry became obsessed with sex at the onset of puberty, which for him happened by age eleven. Throughout his life he kept a sexual journal of every sexual experience he had: with whom, what was done, and how much he enjoyed it. According to his journal, he had sex with over 2000 partners by age 40. As an adult, he had sexual contact with both males and females, several times per week. His wife came to suspect that he might be having sex with their children as well. At this point she sought a divorce and left the country with the children. Jerry left therapy, and closed his practice abruptly. Before any charges could be investigated, he died in a car wreck, under the influence of alcohol.

These cases show different examples of sexual promiscuity and its relation to early childhood abuse. More research and data are necessary for a clearer picture of how childhood sexual abuse is related to adult promiscuity. Of particular importance here is our repeated clinical observations that many cases of adult male homosexual promiscuity are related to incidences of childhood sexual abuse by a male. Further examination is needed before a clear or causal relationship can be defined.

Our clinical experience shows the continuing need by adult survivors of sexual abuse to attempt to master their trauma either by identification with the aggressor which victimizes and uses others, as in Ramon's case; or by re-identification with the early childhood victim leading to revictimization of the self, as with Alan and Jill. The case of Jerry shows victimization both of others and of self.

With increased awareness of the role childhood sexual abuse plays in adult promiscuity, new options for psychotherapeutic treatment are available, offering a shorter intervention time and a more stable recovery period.

REFERENCES

Everstine, D. A., & Everstine, L. (1989). *Sexual trauma in children and adolescents: Dynamics and treatment*. New York: Brunner/Mazel.

Gannon, J. P. (1989). *Soul survivors: A new beginning for adults abused as children*. New York: Prentice-Hall.

Hunter, M. (1990). *Abused boys: The neglected victims of sexual abuse*. Lexington, MA: Lexington Press.

Russell, D. E. H. (1986). *The secret trauma: Incest in the lives of girls and women*. New York: Basic Books.

Timms, R., & Connors, P. (1990). Sexual abuse of young boys: Ending the best kept secret. *VOICES: The Art and Science of Psychotherapy:* 25(4), 57-62.

Addiction or Promiscuity?

Dorothy Litwin

SUMMARY. At one time the terms addiction and promiscuity were clearly defined. Position is put forward that at this time there is a greater degree of understanding of the dynamics of promiscuity whereas the usage of addiction has become far looser and the notion of addiction has burgeoned.

In America sex is an obsession, in other parts of the world it is a fact.

–Marlene Dietrich

The title of this paper is a fitting introduction to the confused state of this field. There was a time when the terms addiction and promiscuity were clearly defined: Addiction was thought of as a physiological and/or psychological dependence upon a chemical substance, the removal of which caused symptoms of withdrawal. Promiscuity described a form of sexual behavior, basically applied to women who were thought of as morally loose because they had many sexual partners. The definitions have changed, and while there is hardly a consensus, and who or what is an addict is being debated, an attempt will be made in this presentation to make some sense of the divergent points of view.

It is my position that there is a greater degree of understanding

Dorothy Litwin, PhD, New York University Graduate School of Arts and Sciences, has a special interest in women's issues. She is in private practice in Larchmont and New York City.

Mailing address: 140 East Garden Road, Larchmont, NY 10538.

This article was originally presented at a panel on "Promiscuity: Humanistic Implications" in August, 1990, Boston, MA.

of the dynamics of promiscuity, less of a value judgment, and not as much of a double standard; that is, men are no longer exempt from being considered promiscuous. The usage of addiction has become far looser: The seriousness of addiction has been diluted and the clinical meaning obfuscated, thus complicating the understanding and treatment of true addictions. While DSM III-R categories are not entirely satisfactory in defining sex disorders, the definitions are more appropriate than for addiction. The term addiction was exclusively reserved for dependence upon substances, but this is no longer the case.

When an article in the business section of *The New York Times* has a subheadline stating, "Addicted to incentives, car buyers must also pay for them," and the writer means that consumers seem to require rebates before they will buy, this reflects the extent to which the concept, loosely used, has trickled down and is being misapplied.

Aided and abetted by the profit motive, some industries have a vested interest in exploiting the notion of addiction. Support for use of addiction comes from several sources. The book industry profits from the proliferation of self-help books on addiction. An enormous popular library is now available which details addiction and which just about incorporates any kind of behavior. Wendy Kaminer (1990), in discussing codependency–also considered an addiction–in *The New York Times* Book Review section, has pointed out that (at that time) *Codependent No More* had been on the paperback best seller list for 90 weeks and had sold over 1.5 million copies. *Adult Children of Alcoholics* by J. Woititz had sold over 1.1 million copies; and the president of Health Communications, a small publisher of this type of book, expected sales to top 3 million in 1990. The essence of these books is basically the same; the prototype addiction is alcoholism and all the other addictions described are variations on the theme of substance addiction. Any one book describes all the addictions and it is a matter of substituting one noun for another in the other books. It is remarkable, therefore, that there is such a demand for so many versions, when any one of these books would suffice. However, publicizing and promoting the notion of an assortment of distinctive addictions can only add to the coffers of the publishing industry, not necessarily to the edification of the public.

Typical of the current crop of authors of self-help literature is Ann Schaef, a prolific writer, who exemplifies the way in which the concept of addiction is currently used. In one of her books called *When Society Becomes an Addict* (Schaef, 1987), she makes a distinction between substance addiction and process addiction: Included in the latter category are addiction to accumulating money, gambling, work, religion, worry, and sex. In fact, as the title of the book suggests, she believes that a person can become addicted to anything, including other people, and that an addiction is a progressive, fatal disease. Based on substance addiction, she has built a theory of sex addiction for which any addiction can be substituted and the assumptions and treatment for all addictions is based on the 12-step Alcoholics Anonymous format. Schaef has a PhD in something unspecified, is a busy lecturer, and has an active private practice treating addictions.

On this score, it is important to point out that addiction business is big business. Rehabilitation institutions have flourished in recent years, and it is now possible to be treated in a multitude of ways: for example, in outpatient private practice, in a clinic, on an individual basis, or in a group of various kinds; in an inpatient setting from 28 days (the number coinciding with what insurance companies will cover), or more, to an institution for the rich in the heart of a big city or in a gorgeous bucolic setting, including rolling hills and ponds. Multinational corporations own some of these institutions and thousands of people are employed in this industry. Of note is that very little good research has been conducted to determine how beneficial these various methods of treatment are.

Another important influence is the tendency of Americans to be faddists so that concepts have a vogue and are then discarded. In my day, schizophrenogenic mother was popular as was the diagnosis of psuedoneurotic schizophrenic, or schizophrenic with decompensating neurotic defenses. Self-actualization was fashionable in the '60s, and currently everybody is getting in touch with their feelings. Safire of *The New York Times* has written a rather amusing column about psychological jargon, particularly focusing on the term "bonding" which has replaced "attachment" and "camaraderie," and now happens between people and animals, not just between people.

In the same vein, Mednick (1989) has discussed constructs which do not hold up to scientific scrutiny but are employed as though they have validity, and, in effect, become cliches. Popularized and used indiscriminately by lay people and professionals alike, such concepts as fear of success, androgyny, and that women have a different "voice" accounting for gender differences in morality, are words which have become trendy, without much thought to applicability. Addiction, as it is used these days, falls into this category.

Upon reflection, it is obvious that people have always conducted themselves in the same sexual patterns. The definitions have changed, not the conduct. Along these lines, Levine and Troiden (1988) state that sexual conduct is culturally determined and reflects moral values of particular societies at particular times. According to Coleman (1986), the prevalence of sexually transmitted diseases, teenage pregnancies, and relatively greater openness of homosexuality have given rise to the invention of normal sexual behavior by conservative religious and political groups. Because moral judgments are attached to sexual behavior, sexual behavior that is considered deviant is being called an addiction and has assumed a pathological diagnosis. At best, the diagnosis of addiction is subjective in terms of the therapist's and/or the individual's perception of the boundary of control. Schwartz and Brasted (1988) consider therapy successful for sex addiction when the individual establishes a healthy, committed, primary relationship with a network of secondary relationships. But as we know, what is mature or normal is also highly subjective.

In contrast, Levine and Troiden suggest, there is an implied value judgment in regard to the conditions under which a mature relationship is achieved; and they question whether this type of traditional solution is a necessary condition for cure. Further, they object to the use of the term addiction with regard to sex because sex is an experience, not a substance, and there are no physiological withdrawal symptoms. Nor, for the same reasons, can they countenance a disease label, or, as has been suggested, accept that insanity is applicable.

At the other end of the spectrum is Carnes (1983), a psychologist, who designed and remains a consultant to a Sexual Dependency Unit as part of a larger institution, which also treats chemical dependency; depression and stress, including phobias and panic;

women suffering from gender-specific depression; crisis treatment; eating disorders; and also offers child and adolescent services. His book *Out of the Shadows* is the authoritative text for sex-addiction practitioners, and, quite obviously, has its roots in substance addiction. Briefly, he compares sex addiction to alcohol addiction because the sex addict uses a mood-altering experience, just as the alcoholic uses a mood-altering drug. The sex addict substitutes a sick relationship for a healthy relationship, whereas the alcoholic has a pathological relationship with a chemical. The sex addict goes through a progressive addictive cycle which becomes increasingly focused on sex. Beginning with Level 1 which includes indulgence in sexually acceptable behavior, for example, excessive masturbation, multiple partners, pornography, patronizing prostitutes; to Level 2 which includes "nuisance offenses," for example, voyeurism, exhibitionism, indecent phone calls, and so on; to Level 3 which includes rape, child molesting, and incest. Carnes believes sex addiction is a progressive disease and that the 12-step program of A.A., slightly modified for sex addicts, is the centerpiece to recovery.

An example of how the notion of addiction has burgeoned is the co-related component of sex addiction, codependency, which is also a direct outgrowth of substance addiction. Since most alleged sex addicts are men, women are labeled "enablers" because they help make the addiction possible. Because enablers (women) are basically dependent people, they become addicted and accede to masculine sexual demands, thus aiding and abetting sex addiction. Kasl (1989) states that codependents permit their bodies to be exploited as they barter sex for relationships and security. Accordingly, because these codependent women are just as addicted as sex addicts, they also benefit from the 12-step A.A. program. Brown (1990) takes exception to characterizing women as addicts and/or to their being blamed as victims. It is as though these women are raped, abused, or subjected to violent treatment because of their addiction and that those not addicted, if there are any according to this point of view, do not suffer from similar treatment. The cause of their dependency becomes translated into an addiction and is attributed to personal, emotional pathology while their subordinate position in society is not considered to be a contributing factor.

Promiscuity is a term which once was exclusively applied to women. Men sowed their wild oats and it was permissible for them to have many partners; in fact, quantity was a measure of masculinity. Weissberg and Levay (1986) found that women do not use sex to enhance their femininity because women who had many partners were considered to be tramps, sick and self-destructive. For women, premarital sex was immoral. The bias of these judgments was accepted as truth; no consideration was given to the fact that for every woman who was involved sexually, with some exceptions, there had to be a man. With the women's movement toward equality, it is now accepted that men's sexual behavior can also be viewed as promiscuous. Simon (1989) concludes that there is a clear sex difference in sexual promiscuity among college students. In an introductory psychology class he surveyed, the number of sex partners males admitted to was 14.6 as opposed to 5.6 for females. Reflecting changing times, McKinney (Klein, 1990) reported that college women who used contraceptives were regarded as supportive of women's rights and not as more promiscuous or as having a bad or loose reputation. However, even with the best of motivation, discrimination along gender lines in this regard continues. Fluker (1983) reports that in his genito-urinary department in London, England, the word promiscuous is banned because each person has a subjective definition. He then goes on to describe various causes of promiscuity, all gender related: unwanted pregnancy, prostitution, wife swapping, and extramarital relationships, with no mention of men. However, with some exceptions, value judgments attached to promiscuity seem to have changed among some groups; while it is accepted that promiscuous behavior exists, there is less of a double standard.

Interestingly, Lieberman (1988) found, in comparing attitudes toward extrapremarital relationships with extramarital relationships among college students, that as long as exclusivity in a relationship was expected, promiscuity was disapproved. This applied to both genders equally. Contrary to common opinion that promiscuous behavior is widespread, it is by no means generally accepted sexual behavior.

According to proponents of sex addiction, promiscuity could be either a cause or a consequence of sex addiction. That is, promiscuous people are sex addicts by virtue of quantity which is deemed excessive. The caveat is with this way of thinking that an acceptable quantity varies with the individual, society, and culture. A case in point would be the Kennedy family. The father, Joe, and his sons, with the exception of Robert who was said to be puritanical in his attitude toward sex, were, and continue to be, notable for their sexual exploits. In fact, Edward's judgment was in question because of his sexual exploits and, at one point, his future political career was on the line. Their promiscuous sex behavior could be used as evidence of a genetic marker for sex addiction, particularly, since it was said that Honey Fitz, the grandfather, also was a womanizer. However, other reasonable explanations are that promiscuity was prompted by the existence of competition among the Kennedy brothers, and/or that in this socioeconomic group, it was as fashionable for men to be involved with many women as it was to have a fancy new car every year.

Perhaps the question would better be answered by examining what the terms sex addiction or promiscuity would add to our present state of knowledge regarding diagnosis, treatment, or theory. DSM III-R includes definitions of psychoactive substance dependence (chemical dependency), obsessive-compulsive disorder, impulse-control disorders, and sexual disorders. Even though there is a great deal of overlapping between categories and these are by no means precise, the categories are more careful in definition and would seem to be better able to diagnose sex disorders than addiction as applied to sex. The term addiction, as it is popularly used, is used so broadly as to apply to any kind of obsession, compulsion, habit, rumination, even preference and practice when used repeatedly, thereby losing its meaning diagnostically and becoming entirely subjective, confusing, to say the least, the treatment process.

For the individual who is troubled by behavior which gets in the way of a well-ordered life, to have a label or an explanation can be comforting. However, there is a danger that explanations of this sort can be accepted as a cause and result in explorations and self-understanding being short circuited. For instance, some justify giving alcohol dependence the dubious label "disease," rationalizing that by removing the moral stigma and guilt the person is more likely to admit to the addiction and obtain help. For some, this is enough to shortstop getting further help beyond A.A., and consequently, the person can then remain in "recovery" forever. That is to say, if treated as an addiction, sex is abstracted from the total personality and treated as though it has a life of its own.

Sex Addicts Anonymous and the 12-step program is generally the core of the help offered for "sex addiction." To my mind it is doubtful if these people are seen as individuals since they are all shunted into the same framework of help and are treated alike. For one thing, the transfer of counseling or therapy training from one addiction to another has to be questioned, as well as the level of training of the counselors, which is inadequate in most cases. While the 12-step program has been helpful for some, it does not work for all. This does not mean the individual is not amenable to another form of treatment, in spite of the position that some advocates of this form of help take. Sometimes, nothing seems to work, most likely because our knowledge is limited and we forget, therefore,[1] that not everyone can be helped.

The grassroots movement of the various self-help sex-addiction groups notwithstanding, that the 12-step program works for some does not support the sex-addiction label. All kinds of therapy work for some people, be it primal scream, rebirthing, electric shock, and so on. However, the fact that it works does not validate the label. Testimonials of the procedure are generally based on anecdotal evidence, not on empirical, objective data. Besides being logically fallacious, this is not an acceptable scientific method.

I end on a cautionary note. Even though the climate is changing regarding promiscuity, the double standard, and certain sexual practices, it is not likely that attitudes have changed among some groups, for example, fundamentalists of various religious persuasions, including the Moral Majority and other politically conservative groups. These groups would have reservations about anything sexual which departs from their version of what is practiced by most Americans. As psychologists, it is important to be aware of the consequences of diagnosing sex as an addiction because the unusual, the deviant, or excessive quantity can become a threat to those who have their own ideas of normal and, therefore, acceptable sexual behavior. If norms for sexual behavior are advocated, the danger is that this will become a standard by which to judge acceptable sexual behavior and morals; minority groups can suffer as targets of the self-righteous standard bearers and individuals would be in jeopardy of forfeiting their civil rights. A case in point is the controversy which surrounded Robert Maplethorpe's work and the question of censorship by Congress and future grants by the National Endowment for the Arts.

NOTE

1. A personal communication from a colleague who practices sex therapy confirms that, at times, she does not know what to do with certain types of sex behavior and has referred some clients to Minneapolis, the addiction center. Coleman (1986) also states that he is "in the dark" with certain paraphilias or with compulsive patterns.

REFERENCES

Barth, R. J., & Kinder, B. N. (1987). The mislabeling of sexual impulsivity. *Journal of Sex & Marital Roles, 13*, 15-23.

Brown, L. S. (1990). What's addiction got to do with it: A feminist critique of codependence. *Psychology of Women Newsletter, Div. 35, APA. 17*, 1, 1-4.

Carnes, P. (1983). *Out of the shadows: Understanding sexual addiction*. MN: Compcare.

Coleman, E. (1986). Sexual compulsion vs. sexual addiction: The debate continues. *SIECUS Report, 14*, 7-11.

Collier, P., & Horowitz, D. (1984). *The Kennedys, an American drama*. New York: Summit Books.

Fluker, J. L. (1983). The perils of promiscuity. *Journal of Psychosomatic Research, 27*, 153-156.

Kaminer, W. (1990, Feb. 11). *Chances are you're codependent too. N.Y. Times Book Review*, pp. 26-27.

Kasl, C. D. (1989). *Women, sex and addiction: A search for love and power*. New York: Ticknor & Fields.

Klein, M. (1990). The emperor's new addiction. *Playboy, 37*, 41.

Koskoff, D.E. (1974). *Joseph P. Kennedy. A life and times*. Englewood Cliffs, NJ: Prentice Hall.

Levine, M.P., & Troiden, R. R. (1988). The myth of sexual compulsivity. *Journal of Sex Research, 25*, 347-363.

Lieberman, B. (1988). Extrapremarital intercourse: Attitudes toward a neglected sexual behavior. *Journal of Sex Research, 24*, 291-299.

Mednick, M. (1989). On the politics of psychological constructs. *American Psychologist, 44*, 1118-1123.

Safire, W. (1990, June 24). The bonding market. *N.Y. Times Magazine*, pp. 12-14.

Schaef, A. W. (1987). *When society becomes an addict*. San Francisco: Harper & Row.

Schaef, A. W. (1989). *Escape from intimacy*. San Francisco: Harper & Row.

Schwartz, M.F., & Brasted, W. S. (1985). Sexual addiction: Self-hatred, guilt, and passive rage contribute to this deviant behavior. *Medical Aspects of Human Sexuality. 19*, 103-107.

Simon, A. (1989). Promiscuity as sex difference. *Psychological Reports, 64*, 802.

Weissberg, J. H., & Levay, A. N. (19). Compulsive sexual behavior. *Medical Aspects of Human Sexuality, 20*, 129-136.

The Concept of Promiscuity: A Self Psychology Perspective

Jeffrey L. Trop
Ronald Alexander

SUMMARY. The purpose of this paper is to demonstrate a self-psychological approach to the understanding of promiscuity. A patient is described who utilized sexual activities as an attempt to acquire affirming and mirroring responses to stabilize her fragile sense of self. A mirroring transference spontaneously unfolded in the treatment which subsequently became eroticized. The selfobject mirroring tie to the therapist gradually became internalized within the patient as she was able to calm and soothe herself. A definition of promiscuity from within a self-psychological framework emerged from this treatment. Promiscuity is the subjective experience of the patient that sexual activities are being utilized primarily to restore and maintain self-cohesion.

It is our intent to examine the concept of promiscuity from the perspective of self psychology. The term promiscuous has the potential to have judgmental and pejorative connotations. We will attempt to reexamine the phenomena of repetitive sexual enactments by illuminating the underlying developmental longings which are

---

Jeffrey Trop, MD, went to the University of California, Los Angeles Medical School and received his training in psychiatry at the Brentwood V.A. Hospital. He is a supervising and training analyst at the Institute of Contemporary Psychoanalysis in Los Angeles. He is Assistant Clinical Professor of Psychiatry, UCLA School of Medicine, 11980 San Vicente Blvd., St. 819, Los Angeles, CA 90049.

Ronald Alexander, PhD, was educated at the University of Massachusetts at Amherst and California State University, Sonoma. He is in private practice in Santa Monica, California, and Chairman of Graduate Psychology and Director of Clinical Training at Riokan College.

embedded in the behavior. A case will be described of a 26-year-old woman who has been in psychotherapy three times per week for 5 years. This patient entered treatment with a history of sexual interactions with a variety of men. The recognition and interpretation of underlying selfobject transference configurations was essential to the therapeutic outcome. We will be emphasizing clinical issues in this paper, but we will briefly review some of the theoretical concepts of self psychology which were useful in this treatment.

Kohut and Wolf (1978) described the essence of selfobject transferences as follows:

> Selfobjects are objects which we experience as part of our self; the expected control over them is, therefore, closer to the concept of the control which a grown-up expects to have over his own body and mind than to the concept of the control which he expects to have over others. There are two kinds of selfobjects: those who respond to and confirm the child's innate sense of vigour, greatness and perfection; and those to whom the child can look up and with whom he can merge as an image of calmness, infallibility and omnipotence. The first type is referred to as the mirroring selfobject, the second as the idealized parent imago. (p. 414)

Atwood and Stolorow (1984), in describing Kohut's contributions, state: "A selfobject may be described phenomenologically as an object that a person experiences as incompletely separated from himself and that serves to maintain his sense of self" (p. 39). They then describe the therapeutic process as follows:

> In the selfobject transferences, the patient revives with the analyst the early idealizing and mirroring ties that had been traumatically and phase-inappropriately ruptured during the formative years, and upon which he now comes to rely for the restoration and maintenance of a sense of self and for the resumption and completion of arrested psychological growth. (pp. 52-53)

Several other authors have discussed the more specific utilization of sexuality as a substitute for self-regulatory capacities. Kohut

(1971,1977) described how sexual activities were utilized to attempt to address feelings of inner deadness in patients who had been deprived of mirroring responses in childhood. Goldberg (1975) described the value of self psychology in understanding perverse behavior. In a previous article on selflessness, Alexander and Trop (1985/1986) described the case of a patient who performed ritualistic sexual activities to compensate for defects of the self.

CASE HISTORY

Gretchen was a 26-year-old female school teacher who came into treatment describing intense feelings of depression, emptiness, and a pervasive feeling of hopelessness. She was not optimistic about being helped by the treatment, but came at the advice of a co-worker who was familiar with her problems. Gretchen came to the first interview dressed in a short skirt with her blouse undone, wearing flashy stockings and heavily made up. She immediately began to tell the therapist about how much pain and unhappiness she was experiencing in her life. She was having an affair with her boss and was deeply distraught over this affair because he was married and had a family. He was therefore unavailable to her except during the day and for short time periods during the weekend.

Gretchen asked if she could use the couch in her therapy so that she wouldn't have to face the therapist as she felt she had terrible things to disclose about herself. She quickly began to tell the therapist in a explicit manner how she and her boss would have sex in the lounge, in elevators both at school and in public office buildings, as well as outside in a variety of settings. She also reported that she would have sex with a variety of other men whom she would pick up at public places. Sometimes she would have sex with three different men in one day or demand sex with her boss at school several times a day.

She was not particularly upset at these sexual activities, but was upset about feeling repeatedly alone as these men would invariably leave her and she would feel intensely empty and abandoned. Her job at school was not satisfying and she only experienced feeling alive and vibrant when she was in the presence of a man who was excited with her. She described how wonderful it felt when she was able to surprise a man by being sexually exciting and then seeing how much men wanted her.

Her history gradually began to unfold over the early months of therapy. She grew up in the southwestern United States, in a simple home with a father whom she described as withdrawn, cold, and over involved in his work. She never remembered having an emotional relationship with him. Her mother was dominant, hyper-critical, and highly abusive. She reported that her mother would characteristically scream at her and also physically beat her. Gretchen was the oldest of four children and had three younger brothers. Gretchen ended up as essentially a maid and servant to assist her mother, and her childhood clearly had a Cinderella-like quality to it. Her mother was totally devoted to her three boys and idealized them. She treated Gretchen with disdain and derision as Gretchen waited on the boys and cleaned their rooms. Her father was also the constant source of his wife's abusive behavior. Later in the treatment Gretchen theorized that her father had thrown himself into business meetings in order to avoid coming home. There were a few times that Gretchen was able to recall her mother reading to her at night and occasionally hugging her. These moments were very rare, however, and were eclipsed by the mother's bizarre and abusive behavior.

The patient remembers noticing as early as she can recall that her mother paraded around the home without clothing and overly displayed her breasts and nude body not only to the family, but specifically in front of workmen who were at the house. When Gretchen began to go through puberty and develop into a woman, her mother frequently went into rageful tirades where she would first assault her daughter with cruel and harsh words specifically focusing upon the "funny little mounds" that Gretchen was developing. The patient would then withdraw with feelings of shame and embarrassment for her body; and her mother would then assault her by slapping and hitting her, screaming obscenities, and at times tearing off the daughter's clothing. Upon further questioning, Gretchen recalled the memory of hearing her mother raging one night to her husband about how the male doctors had castrated her in surgery. Shortly after this episode, the patient was told by her aunt that her mother had undergone a mastectomy for breast cancer. From this point onward the frequency and brutal escalations of these episodes became nearly daily events.

Gretchen described an evolving and repetitive pattern of coping with these repeated attacks. She would retreat to her room and have fantasies of actually being *Cinderella* who would one day eventually be rescued by a prince charming. There were also a wide variety of different rescuers. This included many fantasy male characters including train conductors, policemen, and firemen. All of those male characters had imaginary names, faces, and outfits. Along with these romantic fantasies of rescue, there were also intense sexual fantasies of how she would please these men through offering herself to them sexually. The context of all these fantasies was similar as the patient felt an intense longing "to give," "to pleasure," and to "satisfy" these men in order to obtain their love and approval so that she could feel worthy. Erotic daydreaming and obsessive fantasizing became a daily ritual as a retreat from her mother. At the same time she utilized compulsive masturbation to calm, soothe, and fill up her constant feelings of emptiness and unworthiness.

As her background emerged, it was initially clear to the therapist that her sexual activities were not a source of conflict and guilt for Gretchen. At one point early in the treatment the therapist was more silent than usual when listening to her sexual activities and she became concerned. She told him that she observed his silence and felt he must be thinking how awful she was for engaging in these experiences. She said she knew it was the wrong thing to do. The therapist commented that it appeared that she automatically organized his silence as disapproval. Then in order to reestablish her feeling of connection to him she adopted what she imagined was his negative viewpoint of her sexual activities. Gretchen felt relieved to be understood and said that this was exactly what had transpired and that actually she did not feel conflicted about her sexuality. Her main concern was her pervasive emptiness and depression and her feeling of being alone and forlorn. Thus, at this early juncture in her clinical work, Gretchen clearly did not herself have the inner experience that she was promiscuous from her own vantage point. This was not an issue for her.

Thus, her articulated experience to the therapist that he was thinking her sexual activities were disgusting was not a projection of her own disgust. Rather, she had begun to establish an early mirroring transference to him. She had started to depend on him and his responsiveness to her. When the therapist was more silent, she feared the loss of his selfobject responsiveness. She then unconsciously adopted for herself what she imagined he was feeling in order to revive her tie to him.

As the therapist began to understand more about the meaning of her sexuality he began to make some interpretations about her relationships with men. He commented to her that her sexual activities seemed clearly an attempt to establish some inner feeling of vitality and a sense of being valued. She had established her value by being admired intensely for her capabilities to excite these men. The therapist told her that her self-esteem had been relentlessly undermined by her mother, and Cinderella-like fantasies and sexual activities were reactive attempts to fill in these developmental voids. Thus, her sexual activities were desperate attempts to acquire admiring and mirroring responses to enhance her self-esteem. Gretchen felt very relieved and actually excited about these sets of interpretations. Over the first 2 years of therapy, she continued to have sexual activities with her boss. Her sexual interactions such as picking up men randomly began to diminish significantly. She also began to talk more about other aspects of her life including her work. She did not feel good teaching and began to wonder about other possibilities for herself.

In about the third year of treatment, Gretchen began to develop an increasing capacity to observe herself and her activities. She began to examine her relationship with her boss and started questioning some of his personal qualities. She began to think of him as selfish and was angry that he was seeing two women. She now saw her sexual activities in a different manner. They were not for the purposes of sexual satisfaction but rather were for self-restoration. She knew now that they had clearly developed as attempts to restore a sense of her enfeebled self. She also felt quite anxious at the beginning to think of relationships in terms of what she needed for herself rather than automatically pleasing men. She was afraid she would truly be alone forever. The therapist interpreted these fears as reactions to the changes she was contemplating and he emphasized that they were fears and feelings of being abandoned if she began to mobilize herself around her own agenda. She required the therapist to be very supportive of the changes she was making and the therapist's affirmation of her changes became increasingly important to her.

It was during this third year of treatment that Gretchen gradually mobilized a more intense transference longing. Gretchen asked if she could sit up and have her sessions looking at the therapist in order that she see and feel his responses. She became interested in wanting to know what he thought and felt about her. Prior to this time, most of her material was absorbed in her ritualized sexual acting out with men. It was at this time that she started to experience a desire to have the therapist rescue her from her life so that they live as a couple. Each and every session took up this theme of how empty and emotionally impoverished she felt and how she was fantasizing that they could have been married. She could become free, have a life, and see through him that she was loved and worthwhile. Gretchen said it was essential to her existence to come for treatment so that she could see that look of care and concern in his face that would make her special.

This period of time during the therapy was very intense. The therapist interpreted to Gretchen how she longed to acquire a feeling of specialness by obtaining his affirming and mirroring responses in concrete form. He told her that she feared that this was the only way she could feel valuable. She replied that she knew this was accurate and her longings for him reflected her panic about giving up her sexual activities. This material was worked through over many, many months. The therapist had to repeatedly interpret her longings as responses to her developmental deficits. She had not been mirrored and affirmed during her childhood for any of her unique attributes. Her capacity to excite men was the only previous method she had established to invigorate herself. Thus, her erotized transference arose because she had an underlying desperation about the therapist admiring her for other attributes besides her sexuality. Her sexual fantasies about the therapist gradually receded. She still intensely needed his support, encouragement, and confidence in her process.

Gretchen slowly began to develop a beginning conviction that she could develop some of her other talents and skills. She decided to terminate her affair with her boss. This was very hard for her to do as he argued and begged her to stay with him. He felt quite desperate for her and this tugged at her. She turned to the therapist many times and asked him if he thought she was doing the right thing. He replied that she felt very frightened to give up her old way of acquiring responsiveness and establishing herself around her own unique agendas. She would feel relieved at his comments but required his continued support during this process. As the therapy progressed she did terminate the affair with her boss. She also joined a gym and took up an interest in photography that she had abandoned during adolescence because of her mother. She reported that whenever she would get the "urge" to sexually engage men, she would think of her therapy and begin to feel more worthwhile and remind herself to attend classes at the gym or go and volunteer at the local museum.

During the fourth and fifth years of treatment, Gretchen began to take classes at a nearby art college. One of her teachers who recognized her talent provided her with assistance to enter art school. She subsequently went on to obtain an art degree and teach at a local community college. Shortly after this she began to paint and became intensely absorbed in her painting and photography. Her painting and art became increasingly important to her and she felt increasingly vital. She recalled suppressed memories from her childhood where she had tried to paint and she remembered her mother's scornful responses to her art. Presently she is teaching art at the college level and frequently has showings of her work and is earning an extra income through this artistic endeavor.

She is also dating several men and her sexual activities occur in the context of these relationships. She is still vulnerable to periods of psychological disruption, particularly when the therapist is on vacation. At these times she will develop fantasies of engaging men similar to her past activities. She is able to calm and sooth herself by her understanding that these fantasies are reactive to the temporary absence of the therapist. This awareness has given her the capacity to forestall the need for concrete sexual enactments to stabilize her inner experience.

DISCUSSION

The patient described here had developed a persistent pattern of repetitive sexual enactments with men. The patient had been abused by her mother during her childhood and had retreated to a world of Cinderella-type fantasies in order to calm and sooth herself during her childhood. In these fantasies she used her sexuality as a way of assuring herself that she would be mirrored. Her mother's critical focus on her developing bodily changes during adolescence probably played a pivotal role in shaping the sexual nature of her fantasies.

As she developed into an adult, the patient had clearly evolved an eroticized style to attempt to buttress her fragile sense of self. Thus, the search for eroticized admiring and mirroring responses from men was a substitute for the affirmation and mirroring that she never received as a child. In a previous paper delineating specific aspects of eroticized transference, Trop (1988) stated:

> The eroticization of selfobject needs for mirroring was seen as a response to, and a sexualized substitute for, thwarted mirroring needs. It was also a defensive effort to establish pseudo-mirroring ties via serving an object's sexual wishes. Women or men with this type of personality organization have been repeatedly rebuffed and not recognized for the multiple facets of their personalities, and their sense of being admired has become centered on their physical attractiveness. Their self-esteem is then defensively structured on their continued capacity to engender excitement in the other. When they disappoint someone, they do not have the capacity to maintain a cohesive self. (p. 281)

This patient developed an eroticized transference to the therapist as part of her clinical course. She revived with him both her hope of being mirrored for her sexuality and a fear that this was the only part of her worth admiring. As she worked through the eroticization of her selfobject needs for mirroring, she was able to develop previously buried ambitions. In particular, her capacity for artistic expression had been undermined by her mother during her childhood.

She automatically revived this ambition as she developed confidence in her own intrinsic feeling of value. The eroticized transference and eroticized relationships gradually diminished as her artistic abilities became a source of gratification and aliveness.

This patient illustrates the treatment of the symptom of promiscuity from a self-psychological vantage point. The concept of promiscuity needs redefinition from within this framework. Promiscuity cannot be defined as an objective phenomenon with reference to the frequency and type of sexual contact. In this patient her sexual activities were a developmental substitute for the mirroring responsiveness she did not acquire as a child. In the beginning of the treatment she was not concerned with promiscuity but rather was concerned about feeling empty. As the developmental implications of her sexuality were interpreted to the patient, she gradually developed a mirroring transference to the therapist. She began to develop more confidence and also saw more clearly that her sexual activities were an attempt to validate herself. This facilitated the consolidation of other positive attributes as part of her sense of self such as her artistic abilities. It was at this time that the patient could be said to have developed the inner experience of being promiscuous. She could only achieve this insight after understanding the developmental implications of her sexual activities. We are therefore proposing a new definition of promiscuity using self-psychological principles. Promiscuity is the subjective experience of the patient that sexual activities are being utilized primarily to restore and maintain self-cohesion. This patient acquired this insight within the context of a spontaneous unfolding mirroring transference. The therapist thus served as a bridge whereby structure was acquired as the patient consolidated her capacity to perform self-affirming activities.

In summary, it is our viewpoint that self psychology provides a unique developmental framework for understanding the promiscuous patient. A mirroring selfobject transference will unfold as the patient attempts to acquire mirroring responses from the therapist that were not available during childhood. The diversion of sexual activities as a defensive substitute for structural capacities to maintain cohesion will be experienced from within the subjective world of the patient.

REFERENCES

Alexander, R., & Trop, J. (1985/1986). Self psychology and selflessness: A clinical application. *The psychotherapy patient*, 2(2), 39-47.

Atwood, G., & Stolorow, R. (1984). *Structures of subjectivity, explorations in psychoanalytic phenomenology*. Hillsdale, NJ: The Analytic Press.

Goldberg, A. (1975). A fresh look at perverse behavior. *International Journal of Psychoanalysis, 56*, 335-342.

Kohut, H. (1971). *The analysis of the self*. New York: International Universities Press.

Kohut, H. (1977). *The restoration of the self*. New York: International Universities Press.

Kohut, H., & Wolf, E. (1978). The disorders of the self and their treatment: An outline. *International Journal of Psychoanalysis*, 59, 413-425.

Trop, J. (1988). Erotic and eroticized transference–A self psychology perspective. *Psychoanalytic Psychology, 5*(3), 269-284.

Hypersexuality as a Disorder of the Self

Jerrold R. Brandell
Josephine Nol

SUMMARY. The focus of this paper is the clinical phenomenon of hypersexuality as it is encountered in the psychotherapeutic treatment of adult males. Hypersexuality, it is argued, can be most usefully understood within the theoretical framework of Kohut's psychology of the self. A review of relevant literature, including a brief exposition of the major theoretical premises of self psychology, is presented, along with two clinical examples derived from the authors' psychotherapy practice.

This paper focuses on the clinical phenomenon of hypersexuality as it is encountered in work with the adult male psychotherapy patient. Although hypersexuality is not a gender-bound phenomenon, and may well be observed to occur with some frequency in female as well as in male patients, we have chosen to limit our discussion to male patients for the following reasons. To the degree that sociocultural factors are operative in shaping hypersexual behavior, it appears likely that sanctions against such behavior are differentially reinforced according to gender. The word *promiscuous*, the term used most commonly to characterize indiscriminate sexual encounters, has a pejorative connotation and is applied far more often to women than it is to men. Historically, there has always been greater acceptance of the hypersexual male who is mere-

---

Jerrold Brandell is affiliated with Wayne State University School of Social Work, Detroit, MI 48202.

Josephine Nol, ACSW, is a doctoral student at Smith College School for Social Work. She maintains a private practice in the Hartford area and teaches part-time at the University of Connecticut School of Social Work, 59 Woodchuck Hill Road, West Simsbury, CT 06092.

ly "sowing his wild oats" than there has been for the hypersexual female. We would conjecture that there may well be significant differences with regard to motives and underlying personality dynamics between hypersexual men and women precisely because of the differing sociocultural milieux within which each develops. Another related reason was the difficulty both authors had in identifying female patients who could serve as suitable clinical examples of hypersexuality. We do not make the claim that the clinical examples presented below are *representative* of the hypersexual adult male client population but that they are *illustrative* of certain issues commonly encountered in treating such patients.

HYPERSEXUALITY AND THE STRUCTURE OF THE SELF

In the last 20 years, since the publication of *Analysis of the Self* (Kohut, 1971), Kohut and other adherents of self psychology have transformed this theory into a comprehensive approach to the understanding and treatment of a broad range of psychopathology. Although Kohut initially focused on the understanding and treatment of patients with narcissistic disorders in the narrow sense, self psychology came to be applied with increasing frequency to a very broad range of disturbances, which he called selfobject disorders.

While space does not permit a comprehensive summary of Kohut's theory, a few salient features can be provided. According to self psychology, the critical determinants of psychopathology in both adulthood and in childhood can be traced to gross failures of empathy with one's primary caretakers that occur in childhood. In effect, the empathic failures of parents or parental substitutes need to occur repeatedly and to constitute a chronic and pathogenic pattern of interaction in order for the child to experience them as traumatic. The child's relationship to his or her parents is characterized by *selfobject* needs that, in normal development, result in the formation of intrapsychic structures that take over the selfobject's function through a process Kohut has called *transmuting internalization*. These selfobject needs fall into two basic realms: the need for parental *mirroring*, which is characterized by the parents' capacity to take both pleasure and pride in the child's healthy exhibitionism, in his or her achievements and accomplishments (Kohut & Tolpin, 1980), as well as their capacity to see and to appreciate the child's struggles; and the need for the *idealized* parental selfobject, the parent who can naturally and spontaneously lend the child "security, reassurance, strengthening (and) literally and figuratively uplifting care" which makes the child "feel one with the stable, strong, whole and capable adult" (p. 426). *Transmuting internalization*, a process involving *optimal empathic failures*[1] on the part of the child's parental figures, permits her or him to take in the selfobject functions and attributes and to make them an enduring part of her or his own intrapsychic structure, thereby lessening the need for these external esteem-enhancing supplies.

When there has been a chronic pattern of disappointments in the parental selfobjects, the process of transmuting internalization cannot proceed normally, and the child's (or adult's) self is experienced as noncohesive, fragmentary, and depleted. Kohut and Tolpin (1980), Ornstein (1984), and others have discussed the broad range of psychopathology associated with the failure to achieve a cohesive self structure, and psychoanalytic strategies as well as psychotherapeutic strategies (Baker & Baker, 1987; White & Weiner, 1986) have been extensively discussed in the clinical literature.

Kohut conceived of both sexual "perversions" (e.g., sadism, masochism, and sexual voyeurism) and hypersexuality as disintegration products. That is, such symptoms are a consequence of a faultily functioning or non-cohesive self, and it would be incorrect to view them within the framework of drive theory.

> The behavioral manifestations that appear to be the expression of a primary drive are secondary phenomena. The essence of sadism and masochism, for example, is not the expression of a . . . primary biological drive . . . (but rather) the drive appears as disintegration product. (Kohut, 1978, p. 128)

Goldberg (1975) has suggested that "perverse" erotic experience can be used in the service of mastering painful affects, and Stolorow and Lachmann (1980), following Kohut, have explained how perverse sexual practices may prevent the destabilization of fragmentation-prone self and object representations.

Shapiro (1984) has described the connection between a middle-aged male patient's homosexual fantasies (and associated escalating casual homoerotic encounters) with profound feelings of longing and aloneness of which the patient was barely aware. "Fellatio could provide a sense of contact, a feeling of relief, comfort, and reassurance, a sense of integrity that momentarily relieved the fear of fragmentation" (p. 166). Such homoerotic fantasies and behavior seemed to be clearly linked to underlying structural deficiencies in the idealizing sphere in this particular patient.

In other patients, however, hypersexuality and other unusual sexual practices may signify efforts of the patient to compensate for structural deficiencies in the mirroring sphere, a phenomenon that is illustrated in both of the clinical vignettes that appear below.

The significance of hypersexual behavior in male heterosexuals versus homosexuals, a theme that our own clinical examples raise, is somewhat beyond the scope of this paper. While we do not maintain that there are no important differences linked to sexual orientation, we feel that the similarities are even more compelling and that these are accommodated readily within the theoretical framework of self psychology. In other words, it makes less difference whether a man's hypersexuality is directed toward other men or toward women, if such behavior is fundamentally linked to an underlying pathology of the self.

FIRST CLINICAL EXAMPLE

Leonard was a 32-year-old gay artist who initially sought treatment with his sexual partner, Frank, a garage mechanic in his mid-twenties. Both partners expressed concern over the escalating frequency and intensity of their arguments with each other which had begun several months earlier, shortly after Frank moved in with Leonard. These combative exchanges seemed to center on Leonard's contentions that Frank was continuing to engage in sexual liaisons outside of their relationship without Leonard's permission. Although Frank expressed a desire to maintain his relationship with Leonard, he also candidly admitted to having a competing desire to continue sexual affairs with several other lovers. The idea that Frank might be involved in such liaisons with other partners was actually less disturbing to Leonard than the thought that these sexual encounters might occur outside his awareness. Leonard experienced massive anxiety and profound rage whenever he contemplated this possibility.

In an individual session, Frank indicated that he had "seriously considered" ending his relationship with Leonard for some time, feeling that he needed more independence than Leonard seemed able to allow him in their relationship. In a separate interview, Leonard told the therapist that he, himself, sought anonymous sexual encounters, often with multiple partners, virtually every weekend. Some of these experiences occurred when he and Frank "hit the bars" together, but Leonard also entered into such sexual "threesomes and foursomes" on nights when Frank was working late or spending time with friends. On those occasions, it was a feeling Leonard alternately described as a "horrible boredom" or "a sick, empty kind of feeling" that seemed to propel him out of the house.

After several joint meetings and a series of individual interviews with Leonard and Frank, the therapist recommended individual treatment for both partners, with additional couple counseling to follow at a later date. Since the therapist's involvement with Leonard was considerably more extensive (Frank left treatment after only six interviews), his treatment will be the focus of the clinical vignette that follows.

Leonard was the third in a sibship of four children. He had two older sisters and a younger brother. His earliest memory was of biting off a portion of his tongue as the result of an "accident" at the age of 18 months. Leonard described himself as "accident-prone" throughout his childhood. Only much later did he reveal that many of these accidents were actually incidents during which he was severely physically abused by one or both of his parents, and even then he minimized the "abusive" nature of such events. Leonard described his mother as a domineering and controlling woman who prevailed over the entire household. Even Leonard's father called her "Mommy" when addressing her. Both parents also drank heavily at times, and Leonard at length came to see this as an important factor contributing to the physical abuse both he and an older sister experienced within the family. When he was an infant, Leonard's mother routinely strapped him to his high chair and force-fed him until he would begin to choke on his own vomitus. She later made him wear a leash and a harness whenever she took him out, a practice that continued until he was 4 years old.

Leonard's father, who died when Leonard was 23 years old, was described as "weak and ineffectual." It was this same parent, however, whom Leonard observed to take a sadistic pleasure in slapping and otherwise inflicting pain and humiliation upon him. Leonard's relationship with his father was a distant one, and he had difficulty recalling anything that the two ever did together that was mutually enjoyable. On the other hand, his relationship with his mother never had any spatial or psychological distance, and he often felt that he would never fully escape her influence. When he was a toddler, she frequently dressed him in little girl's clothes, and for a time he even participated in an older sister's Brownie Troop. He recalled that adults often compared him favorably to his older sisters, describing him as a "beautiful child." His mother and her sister often observed to Leonard and to each other that he "should have been born a girl." He found that as early as age three or four, he was able to receive much more attention from his female relatives by "acting like a girl," something he became increasingly adept at doing.

When Leonard was five, his younger brother was born, and he felt that his mother subsequently "turned away" from him so that their relationship was "never really the same." In the same year, Leonard's maternal grandfather died. This loss was a traumatic one for Leonard, since this was the only rewarding relationship with an adult male that he recalled having had as a child.

Leonard's artistic abilities developed early, so that by the time he was 9 or 10 years old, these talents were well recognized both by peers and to a lesser extent by family members. It was particularly important for him to receive affirmation from his mother, although she was rarely enthusiastic about his work, and seemed to take his talent "for granted" most of the time. Leonard's father became interested in his son's artistic ability many years later, and his interest was typically aroused only by the prospect of Leonard selling a given work. As an adult, Leonard has entered literally hundreds of competitions, often placing at or very near the top. Each time, he has experienced a momentary feeling of pleasure, but just as invariably, the glow rapidly fades, and he becomes acutely aware of intolerable feelings of inner desolation and despair.

Although most of his sexual relationships have been with men, Leonard feels that he has always been able to achieve greater intimacy in friendships with women. He has had a long series of close platonic friendships with women whom he describes as intelligent, attractive, and artistically inclined. These relationships, however, seem to follow an all-too-familiar and predictable scenario. Usually the woman finds Leonard to be irresistible, talented, and engaging; his work unusual and provocative. He will bask in her open admiration and appreciation of his talent. While this usually lasts for a while, eventually his new friend will experience his demands for attention, admiration, and interest as insatiable. He will make frantic efforts to hold on to the relationship, but these attempts are rarely successful, and he experiences the subsequent loss of such friendships as a profound injury to his narcissism. Leonard actually reports having had over 25 such friendships since late adolescence.

In therapy, Leonard developed an intense transference that was organized along mirroring lines. Whenever the longed-for admiration or interest that he sought from the therapist (a man) was not forthcoming, he would become characteristically petulant, haughty, and aloof. He was particularly inclined on these occasions to enter into sexual liaisons with multiple partners, which he would later report to the therapist in an embarrassed and self-critical way. He was gradually helped to see that the experience of not being "mirrored" by the psychotherapist recapitulated the early, traumatic failures of maternal attunement with his age-appropriate expressions of ebullience and self-confidence. Such experiences had always left him feeling weak, empty, and psychologically anesthetized, and he had typically engaged in anal or genital masturbation (and as an adolescent, in homosexual liaisons) to counteract these intolerable sensations.

On several occasions early in treatment, Leonard expressed the desire to show the therapist recently completed works of art. The therapist felt that his refusal to agree to these requests, which were made with increasing urgency, actually began to threaten the viability of the therapy. With great reluctance, the therapist consented to see Leonard's work. The following session, he arrived with 5 or 6 sketches of erotic male nudes. The therapist's initial reaction was that of vague discomfiture; and the thought that he had perhaps made a tactical error in agreeing to see the pictures aroused a certain degree of anxiety. The therapist was still somewhat troubled after the hour, but gradually came to an understanding of what had occurred during this session. Leonard's "exhibition" was a poignant expression of a profound need both to experience himself and to be experienced as fully alive and as having a unified body-mind-self. The therapist's willingness simply to view the pictures (without any further valuation or other reaction to them) established for Leonard that the therapist understood the depth of his need to be affirmed. Furthermore, it demonstrated that the therapist was interested not only in the pathological parts of his personality but in the creative parts as well. Following this critically important hour, Leonard made no subsequent requests to bring in additional sketches or other art works. He did invite the therapist to a major exhibition of his work at a well-known midwestern gallery, but this occurred much later in his treatment. It was handled interpretatively by referring to the reawakening of his old fears of others being unresponsive to his need for affirmation and empathic interest, and this interpretation was fairly effective.

After about one year of therapy, Leonard was involved in sexual encounters with multiple partners far less often than he had been during the first several months of treatment.[2] By this time, Frank had moved out, and the two saw each other only occasionally. Leonard was saddened by this lost, but seemed to respond to it with an equanimity that probably would not have been possible earlier in treatment.

SECOND CLINICAL EXAMPLE

Bill, an attractive but disheveled 35-year-old man with a history of violence and drug and alcohol abuse, initially sought treatment for a conflictual relationship with a woman and because of his fears that his alcohol use was the source of the problem. When the therapist was clear with him that treatment was contingent upon his abstinence from drugs, he agreed readily. He reported having had residential and outpatient treatment for alcohol problems and that he had been denied reentry by two different programs when he had been unable to stay sober. His experiences with AA were troubling to him since he felt rejected by members of several local groups who had apparently grown exasperated with him and told him to come back only after he could make a commitment to his sobriety. According to Bill, although he acknowledged that alcohol was indeed part of the problem, there was another issue which seemed more troubling to him. He then began to talk about his relationship with his female partner as the cause of the conflict that led him to drink. The therapist was aware almost immediately of feeling quite protective toward this client, and of experiencing the client as fragile and easily damaged.

Early in the treatment both Bill and Nora (his partner) attended a session together. Nora was vocal and highly anxious during this session. She complained bitterly about Bill's lack of "consideration" for her, and how difficult he made her life by not contributing as much as she thought he should. Bill appeared to struggle between wanting to defend himself from her and trying not to provoke displeasure in the therapist. Nora, who worked as a licensed practical nurse, was also in school pursuing an RN degree. She too was in therapy and had been diagnosed with a bipolar condition for which she took medication. Both spoke with pain about their disappointments in the other. Nora also expressed her fears about Bill's anger, which had led him to hit her in the past. Bill acknowledged this as a problem and tearfully expressed his desire for a solution to his profound unhappiness. He added that part of the pain was Nora's withdrawal from him. Nora was not interested in discussing her possible contributions to the difficulty, nor in participating in further sessions. She said that it was Bill who had the problems and made it very clear that, in her opinion, it was he who had to make the changes if the relationship was to last.

During the next several sessions Bill talked about major arguments between him and his partner that would end in her humiliating him and then withholding affection and sex. This in turn would send him into a helpless rage tinged with a sense of panic. Sometimes when he left the house after an intense argument he would seek out a sexual encounter with a male partner. At this point he spoke with shame about his fear that he might be homosexual. Often he would either masturbate compulsively or seek out a woman on the street to whom he would expose himself. Later, in discussing this issue, he revealed that he had been arrested several times for indecent exposure over a period of 15 years. These exposure incidents had occurred in areas where there was a good possibility that he would be seen, such as in stores or in busy shopping districts.

Several months into the treatment Bill introduced a fear that his penis was too small. He also observed that he had a tendency to share this information with the women with whom he became involved. This fear led him to consult with a physician who he reported had confirmed that his genitals were indeed "smaller than average." Inevitably his partners would use this information during an argument to hurt and further humiliate him.

During these discussions about his genital size, the therapist, who was female, became aware of her feelings that the client wanted her to ask him to expose himself in the office. Rather than a sexual invitation, this seemed to her more like a small boy asking for comfort and reassurance that he was acceptable. Although the feelings generated in the therapist were uncomfortable, she sat with Bill and attended to his pain and shame and his need to be seen. The therapist experienced Bill as being excruciatingly sad and frightened during this particular session. Bill expressed a great fear that he could not sexually please a female partner even as he felt a compulsion to have sexual contact with her. Later he remembered an incident with his mother when he was much younger. In this memory, while she was washing him he got an erection and she laughed at him, ridiculing him about the "smallness" of his genitals. One must speculate on how close this woman had to get to him to "see" his genitals since she was apparently almost blind.

Using the self-psychological lens, Bill can be understood to be suffering from a fragmentary self structure, with serious deficits in both lines of development. His transference-based invitation to the therapist to engage in sexual voyeurism is usefully understood as an attempt to use the therapist as a mirroring selfobject. Bill was poignantly seeking her confirmation and admiration of his capacities. As the therapist continued to sit and to listen to his emerging shame and despair, she became an idealized selfobject by which he could feel soothed and understood.

Both the public and private masturbation activity were designed to provide tension regulation and self-soothing in the face of what he experienced as threats to his psychic integrity. Whenever someone, including the therapist, would do something that he perceived as withholding of selfobject functions (mirroring and idealizing) he would suddenly become enraged and sullen. As the therapist acknowledged the hurt as the source of the rage, his anger would just as quickly abate. Gradually in the treatment, the therapist was able to help him understand the connections between his mother's cruelty, his father's indifference to him, and his need to evoke expressions of pride, pleasure, and sensitivity in his parental selfobjects. When such expressions were not forthcoming it created a hunger that he often acted out sexually.

As Bill's narrative gradually unfolded it began to reveal clues to his sexually charged symptoms and to the responses induced in the therapist. Bill's parents were both approaching middle age when he was born. His father was completely blind while his mother, as noted previously, had severely limited vision. Bill, who was the youngest of four children, described his relationship with both parents as highly conflictual. Gradually a picture emerged, of an impoverished family, struggling along on the meager income his father made at the newsstand job. He talked about severe beatings interspersed with rather raw psychological cruelty. His engagement in a series of petty crimes served to support his parents' extremely negative assessments of him. During adolescence he was labeled incorrigible. He often spoke of his own aggressive rages toward his parents while still living at home with them, and his conviction that he must be profoundly bad to have behaved in such a manner. One vivid memory that he had early in treatment was of being sent away to a home for boys when he was twelve. There he was befriended by an older male who sexually seduced him.

He described his father as authoritarian and painted a picture of a man who not only was literally unable to "see" his son, but who was emotionally unavailable to him and to his mother. He could not recall a single memory of enjoyable times with his father and spoke only vaguely of his mother as an occasional comforting presence. As the therapy evolved he then began to remember angry physical and verbal battles between his parents, often about money. As he explored this the reality of this family's struggles became clearer. His mother, a woman with limited opportunity, had married a rigid, embittered man who offered little financial security. Because of this she suffered loneliness and poverty. It seems that Bill's mother, in her anger and isolation from her husband, often turned to her son to soothe her own narcissistic pain.

Bill did poorly in school, never graduating from high school, and was unable to hold a job. In fact, in a much later session, he shamefully revealed that he couldn't read. He drifted from one unskilled position to the next, often losing the job after an angry outburst at the boss. He became involved in a series of relationships with women who would be doing adequately on their own but who did not have any additional resources to offer him. He could attract women through his handsome physical countenance, but would become frantic when they could not fulfill his almost insatiable sexual appetite. Just before entering treatment Bill had relinquished all parental rights to his 7-year-old son simply because his ex-wife had demanded it. This marriage had disintegrated as a result of his violence toward her and his inability to provide much financial support. He had little contact with his son since the end of this relationship. His lack of ambition and commitment to regular work, as well as his sense of shame and his need to hide himself, also illustrate the extensive damage Bill had sustained in the mirroring sphere.

Many of Bill's sexualized symptoms were understood by the therapist to indicate a disturbance in his mirroring selfobject sphere. When Bill invited the therapist to engage in sexual voyeurism, through the transference, he was using the therapist as a mirroring selfobject. Because the therapist could also sit, listen, and tolerate his shame-filled despair, she became an idealized selfobject through which he could feel calmed and reassured. After one-and-a-half years of treatment, Bill was able to give up the symptom of public masturbation. He was also able to enter a tutoring program to improve his reading skills, evidence of developing self-esteem. Further, Bill began to speak enthusiastically about the real possibility of completing a high-school equivalency program. Other signs of improvement included attainment of a job in lawn maintenance which he was still holding after 8 months, as well as increased attention to his appearance.

CONCLUSION

Both clinical cases presented offer examples of how a self-psychological approach can be useful in the treatment of certain hypersexual conditions in adult males. Inasmuch as psychoanalytically informed treatment relies heavily on the handling of the transference, Kohut's contributions to our understanding of this aspect of the relationship provide us with a helpful framework within which to untangle the often highly charged content of the work with patients suffering from hypersexuality. In these cases, the symptoms were not considered to be rooted in instinct but rather as disintegration products created by damage sustained in selfobject bonding during childhood. The treatment relationship reevoked those conditions and provided an opportunity for reworking, mourning, understanding, and rebuilding, with considerable alleviation of both patients' symptoms.

NOTES

1. Kohut (1984) defines optimal failures as "the (psychotherapist's) unavoidable, yet temporary and thus non-traumatic, empathy failures in the selfobject transference."

2. Since the risk of contracting AIDS was by this time clearly linked to such high-risk sexual behaviors, this lifestyle change may well have had very far-reaching ramifications for Leonard.

REFERENCES

Baker, H. (1971). Heinz Kohut's self psychology: An overview. *American Journal of Psychiatry*, *144*(1), 1-9.

Goldberg, A. (1975). A fresh look at perverse behavior. *International Journal of Psycho-Analysis*, *56*, 335-342.

Kohut, H. (1971). *Analysis of the self.* New York: International Universities Press.
Kohut, H. (1978). *Restoration of the self.* New York: International Universities Press.
Kohut, H. (1984). *How does analysis cure?* Chicago: The University of Chicago Press.
Ornstein, A. (1981). Self-pathology in childhood: Developmental and clinical considerations, *Psychiatric Clinics of North America, 4*(3), 435-453.
Shapiro, S. (1984). Archaic selfobject transferences in the analysis of a case of male homosexuality. In P. Stepansky and A. Goldberg (Eds.), *Kohut's legacy: Contributions to self psychology* (pp. 164-77). Hillsdale, NJ: The Analytic Press.
Stolorow, R.D., & Lachman, F.M. (1980). *Psychoanalysis of developmental arrests.* New York: International Universities Press.
White, M., & Weiner, M. (1986). *The theory and practice of self psychology.* New York: Brunner/Mazel.

"Psychopathological Promiscuity" and "Refinding" in the Quest for Sexual Love: Recapitulations of Incest Fantasy and Narcissism

Robert A. Mednick

SUMMARY. It is proposed that contrary to conventional definitions of "promiscuity" which include the criteria of frequent nonselective sexual intercourse having no plan or purpose, psychoanalytic treatment of "pathological promiscuity" revealed both selectivity and purpose to this behavior. Aspects of the life and treatment of a woman who presented promiscuity and suicidal impulses as her initial problems are presented. Understanding the unconscious determinants of the patient's "refinding" process along with the intrapsychic narcissistic functions which her promiscuity sought to serve underscored the paradox of the definition, and were considered necessary to advance the therapeutic process. An alternate definition of pathological promiscuity is used which recognizes the need for the addition of considerations of intrapsychic conflict, and the psychic functions of narcissistic enactments.

For purposes of psychotherapeutic understanding and treatment it seems necessary and practical to place considerations of "promi-

---

Robert Mednick, PhD, is a faculty member and supervisor at the Institute for Psychoanalysis and Psychotherapy, Postgraduate Center for Mental Health, New York City. He specializes in adult, child, marital, and family psychotherapy and psychoanalysis. He has published widely on topics including repression, sexual fantasy, supervision in psychotherapy, developmental arrest, narcissism, adoption and infertility, resistance, anxiety, and psychological development. He is in private practice in New York City, and at 48 Glenwood Road, Scarsdale, NY 10583.

scuity" into the context of developmental strivings toward a sexual love relationship which we all share in common.

The individual's psychological evolution toward an enduring sexual love relationship is a quest set in motion by the imperatives of our biological and psychodevelopmental heritage (Freud, 1905/1961, 1923/1961, 1931/1961; Bergmann, 1987). With numerous trials and tasks set before us from infancy and at the crossroads of childhood and adolescence, including typical and atypical traumata (A. Freud, 1967), "calamities of childhood" (Brenner, 1982), in addition to "strong forces" at work against an exclusive attachment to one person in adulthood (Eissler, 1963, p. 661), we are hurled into this quest.

Out of this arduous developmental journey we are thus, in adulthood, bestowed with specific predispositions in loving and relating (A. Freud, 1965), especially from the impacts of our developmental passage through the inevitable domains of childhood incestuous fantasy and narcissism.

In fact, we are told that fixations at these areas of psychic development "threaten the love of every human being" (Bergmann, 1987, p. 168). While the genesis of all symptoms is overdetermined (Waelder, 1930), incestuous and narcissistic fixations can contribute significantly to the organization of various symptom complexes. One eventual symptom manifestation may be referred to as "psychopathological promiscuity."[1]

Similar to the definition of promiscuous which emphasizes "*nonselective* sexual intercourse" (English & English, 1958, p. 413; italics mine), Webster (1968) defines promiscuous as "engaging in sexual intercourse *indiscriminately* or with many persons. . .(and) *without plan or purpose*" (italics mine) (p. 1137).

In the following considerations of the theory of "refinding" and the recognition of intrapsychic functions which are served by narcissistic enactments, the examination of promiscuity reveals a paradox in which the descriptive criteria that define promiscuous are contradicted. The clarification of this paradox has important implications for treatment, especially with regard to the pathogenic fixations of incestuous fantasy and narcissism upon which I shall focus.

Freud's (1905) assertion that "the finding of an object is in fact a refinding of it" (p. 222) has been regarded "as Freud's most profound contribution to love" (Bergmann, 1987, p. 159). The manner in which the refinding process unfolds in the presence of psychopathology theoretically should follow a particular *precondition.* Specifically, in the absence of psychopathology "the adult love object always (unconsciously) recalls the infantile one, but the person is free to select a *large number of traits* of the infantile love object" (Bergmann, 1987, p. 164; italics mine). Conversely, in the presence of psychopathology the range of choice is significantly narrowed. This preconditional *narrowing of choice* of the sexual love object, in the presence of psychopathology, seems to contradict the dictionary definitions of promiscuity with regards to the criterion of nonselectivity.

The psychological use of the body, especially sexual activity, and the nature of engagement in relationships has been seen to serve a variety of crucial intrapsychic functions (Kohut, 1971; Lichtenstein, 1964; A. Reich, 1960). Drawing upon this earlier work, Stolorow and Lachmann (1980) advance a definition of narcissistic behavior which considers narcissistic disturbance as a "*dimension of psychopathology* which cuts across all the traditional nosological entities" (p. 23). This definition identifies the unique *functions* served by narcissistic activity including efforts to maintain self-esteem, to establish a stable sense of identity, and to preserve the fundamental organization of the personality (p. 10).

In the psychoanalytic treatment of a patient I shall discuss, it was revealed that the descriptive criteria of the aforenoted definitions of promiscuity are contradicted. In this case, not only did psychopathological promiscuity involve a particular kind of discrimination or selectivity, albeit unconscious, it also involved prime moving *intrapsychic purpose.* To illustrate this paradox and examine fixations on incestuous fantasy and narcissism in pathological promiscuity, I will discuss aspects of the life and psychoanalytic treatment of a woman I shall call Helen who suffered from a chronic compulsion to engage in sexual intercourse resulting in two abortions along with serious contemplations of killing herself.

THE STRUGGLE THROUGH INCESTUOUS FANTASY

Helen was a bright, articulate, and tall 28-year-old attractive single woman when she entered treatment following her second abortion. With embarrassment and a punitive, intense sense of shame she revealed her "uncontrollable" sexual involvements with men which began to escalate after her graduation from college. She indicated that while she was "very certain" about marriage, she desperately wanted to change the way she related to men because of her sense of danger in these activities, and "the way it hurts me." Helen said her problem was not that she was unable to "say no," but rather that "something comes over me, like I go into a cloud."

It seemed manifestly clear to Helen that her selection of men, often two in the same evening, was indiscriminate, except for the fact of their availability. She reported that the cycle of her "messing around" (occasionally Helen used the term promiscuous, but typically as a vehicle for expressing sarcastic anger or defiance against herself or me) followed a general scenario. After a week of suffering from the "last weekend" of multiple sexual involvements with different men, Helen would resolve to either go out with "safe friends" or go out alone "just to get out." She would further resolve to not drink at all, or just minimally. She said she felt she needed to "hold on to something," envisioned herself holding on to a glass of wine, which led to more drinking as her resolve for control gave way to a deeper and more compelling force.

As Helen began to fill in the picture of her troubled quest for sexual love, she revealed that while in college and away from home she had dated in a planned, preparatory, and discriminating manner, selecting only men who were from distinctly different cultural, religious, and racial backgrounds from her own. This appeared as an abiding and necessary precondition of her planned dating. While away at college, Helen seemed to require her sexual partners to be significantly different from any outward physical approximation to herself or her parents. Helen was an only child.

Upon returning home from college, she moved back into her parents home for a brief period, "for convenience sake." Graduating from college, returning home, and anticipating uncertainty about her adult engagement with her life all contributed to Helen's renewed struggle with separation. She said she wanted to be like her friends who "had their own places." Her return home, the anxiety-filled vision of her life before her, and her struggles with separation all served–as we later discovered–to revive the intensity of Helen's long-standing fantasized incestuous tie to her father, as will become clear. Her renewed separation anxiety was central in unconsciously motivating Helen to selectively seek out and create a long series of multiple sexual relationships where the men, to Helen, were essentially anonymous and "faceless."

In Helen's consciously planned dating, typically three or four different men in a week, she repetitiously would quickly "grow out" of her boyfriends, usually prompted by the feeling that they had disappointed or betrayed her in some way, even though she believed she frequently created these feelings "just to get away." Early in treatment, Helen saw no importance or meaning in the fact that she would consistently get the men's names confused, or exchange one name for another, feeling a need to justify this experience by saying "They're all the same anyway!" In her sexual involvements with the anonymous men, she reported feeling confused about her suffering from feeling guilty: "I don't know why I feel it's bad what I do–the men don't mind–but I feel bad inside anyway." Helen said she hated herself for feeling that she was "bad," and that just prior to her calling me for her first appointment she seriously thought about killing herself.

The course of Helen's treatment is remarkable in several ways. At the conclusion of the second initial consultation session, Helen said she was "feeling better" and had decided not to continue. While my recommendations did not support her decision, she simply thanked me in a casual, perfunctory manner for "listening to her," as she addressed me in leaving by mistakenly using the name of her internist.

Two months later Helen returned, but again only for a brief period. This repetition occurred four times during the course of Helen's five-and-a-half-year treatment.

After one year of weekly sessions I recommended psychoanalysis. Helen had begun to demonstrate both a capacity and an important interest in how her feelings and ideas about me were informative about her life. However, three sessions following my recommendation Helen again abruptly discontinued. In a brief telephone follow-up Helen said she felt afraid and needed to be "alone for a while." When she returned once again, this time Helen had become convinced that her comings and goings reflected important meanings as to the nature of her symptoms. First, she told me that, surprisingly to her, she had abruptly stopped seeing men altogether. Then she reported that she had left because the idea had come to her that I reminded her of her gynecologist, that this was stimulating to her, and that she felt she could never tell me. Helen then revealed for the first time that as a very young girl she had become preoccupied with looking at her father's pornographic magazines which were "all over the house," adding that this circumstance was "never brought up" in the family. At that point Helen voluntarily "brought up" wanting to "try" psychoanalysis, but that she still felt frightened. As we began to explore her fears, I recommended modified psychoanalysis (Bernstein, 1983; Rothstein, 1986) which evolved into the standard psychoanalytic situation at about the third year of treatment.

The further unveiling of Helen's history revealed scenes of childhood in which a very intense fantasy relationship with her father prevailed. This enmeshment developed out of chronic pathogenic overstimulation from the father's pornographic magazines along with Helen's highly elaborate fantasy life involving sexual ideas, wishes, and fears about her father. Helen recalled childhood "games" in which she repetitiously enacted the fantasies of "sneaking" to look at her father's magazines. She imagined her father "looking at me looking," and "catching me."

During the third year of treatment, shortly after we had resumed sessions following a holiday vacation, a particularly revealing transference experience unfolded. Helen began to experience disturbing emotional shifts between soothing experiences that she felt "I know myself the more you know me," to the dread behind her defensive rage at me for her feeling that she was "being too close." On several occasions, at times screaming "Get away from me!", these experiences included Helen storming out just before the end of the session, slamming the door. In the sessions which followed these upheavals, Helen returned expressing feelings of embarrassment and guilt, and wishing for "forgiveness."

These enactments were interpreted as expressive of Helen's wish that she would have been protected from the impact of her exposure to the stimulation by her father's magazines as she was trying to protect herself in the revival of this distress in the transference by leaving the sessions. Upon interpreting further that her "leavings" just before the end of sessions were recreations of her feelings of abandonment by her parents in their ignoring Helen, she made two revelations. First, Helen disclosed the fact that at age six she had undergone surgery for a congenital umbilical hernia, and that she magnified the discomfort of this hernia to summon her mother's interest and attention. Secondly, Helen reported that it was after her surgery that she realized her fantasies had changed. In her conscious sexual thoughts, Helen became the *observer* in fantasized scenes where she would witness her father or "some faceless man" sexually involved with some "unknown woman."

After a brief period following Helen's surgery, her father apparently suffered a series of financial failures. He began to drink heavily and became alcoholic. Helen began to have an avalanche of painful memories of finding her father stuporous, fearing and wishing that he were dead. The childhood experiences condensed in her refrain about her father that "He was there but he wasn't. It's like he became somebody else I didn't know" became a significant shaping force which predetermined an unconscious characteristic of "the man" in Helen's life. This trait became a central infantile prototype directing her "refinding" in a sought-after love object in adulthood.

Helen's mother, who appeared largely as a background figure and specifically significant in this regard, was remembered as "always working," but who would eventually become available when Helen was sick or injured. Both Helen and her mother installed a specific condition of togetherness. Helen had to be sick, defective, and dependent; and her mother would be present. In addition, Helen enlisted her defensive imperative that she conceal and deny a sexualized representation of herself in the presence of her mother and father because of their pathogeneity and the dangers of her evolving incestuous fixation. The impact of these experiences on Helen's psychic development became the genesis of her adult symptoms of depersonalization and pathological promiscuity. These symptoms in adulthood repeated the nature of Helen's relationships with her parents in childhood.

Central to Helen's treatment was the evolution of her transferences. These experiences were structured around nodal sexual fantasies which transformed as treatment proceeded. During the initial phase of therapy, Helen would organize herself around me in ways which she fantasized would assure her being "liked," "chosen," and "most preferred of all." As she later revealed, this included the ways she dressed, the style and cadence of her speech, as well as the content of her presentations. The initial dynamic form of her relationship with me was thematized in an early fantasy in which she was "a little girl, my leg is deformed, I can't walk, and some man is rescuing me while we're having sex."

At about the third year of treatment, during a period in which her earlier abrupt halting of promiscuous behavior was attendant to intensifying fears of dating because of expectations of rejection and unbearable loss, she unveiled a new masturbation fantasy. This fantasy was disclosed at a point when she had experienced some relief from the disturbing emotional transference shifts in sessions between feeling soothed and defined ("I know myself the more you know me") at one point, and then intensely anxious ("being too close") at the next: "It's cloudy and dark, and you're having sex with me, but I'm calling you dad."

Working through Helen's transference with the understanding of the multiple meanings of her fantasies required the discovery of her unconscious refinding process and the reconciliation of the narcissistic functions served by her sexual practices.

UNCONSCIOUS SELECTIVITY IN "REFINDING" AND THE NARCISSISTIC FUNCTIONS OF PATHOLOGICAL PROMISCUITY

The transformation in Helen's sexual fantasies from the little girl with the deformed leg to the directly incestuous version in the transference has specific implications. It reveals the secrets of Helen's refinding process where she unconsciously selected men reminiscent of her father. It shows as well the unique defensive purposes and narcissistic functions of her promiscuity.

Selectivity in Refinding

It was in the transference context of Helen's shifts between soothingly feeling known and anxiety about closeness followed by interpretations of her wishes to have been protected (as she was trying to protect herself by storming out of sessions) that Helen first disclosed her memories of her umbilical hernia surgery at age six. Her memories and associations to her surgery clarified a wide range of childhood conflicts including her experience of surgery as punishment for her incestuous fantasies, and the anesthesia as a prototype to her adult depersonalization. In the symptom of "being in the cloud" Helen unconsciously relived her childhood suffering for her sense of guilt, the calling for the presence of her mother, and the wished-for connection with her father by identification, that is, she could be with her father by being like him: stuporous, different, and unknown.

The fact that Helen's childhood sexual fantasies shifted from the imagined participant to the observer after her surgery illuminated the central meaning of her transference reaction of emotional shifts and storming out of sessions. While Helen felt soothed in feeling known, this revived not only the childhood fantasy experiences of her father looking at her looking (if I knew her that meant I was looking at her), but more terrifyingly it placed her subjectively in the incestuous position where she anticipated penetration.

As a defense against the fear of incestuous penetration–Helen's association was the surgeon's knife–she had, in childhood, disassociated herself from the more dangerous incestuous fantasy by installing herself as the observer. In adulthood her defensive disassociation extended to the psychic requirement of becoming unknown and oblivious in her depersonalization symptoms which were a prerequisite of her promiscuity.

Helen's childhood fantasy of observing the sexual engagement of some faceless man and some unknown woman was unconsciously reenacted in her adult sexual experiences. *A precondition of her refinding process required that the man be unknown.* The association to her father in his drunken stupors, as "he became somebody else I didn't know," was the selective trait which Helen had to go to great lengths to recreate in her refinding. This selective refinding requirement for Helen necessitated either that the man bear the greatest dissimilarity to her father, or that there be large numbers of men in which both the sexual overstimulation of childhood and the characteristic of father as "identity unknown" could be preserved.

Narcissistic Functions of Pathological Promiscuity

In contradistinction to the conventional view of promiscuity which defines this behavior as without plan or purpose, understanding the nature of Helen's sexual involvements revealed the desperate purposes at work which dictated her behavior.

Helen's early childhood experiences of psychological abandonment by her largely absent mother effected a deeply disturbing insecurity and anticipation of repetitious object loss. Anticipations of object loss were reflected in Helen's comings and goings during the first year of treatment. This danger was shown as well in her urgency to establish a particular therapeutic tie where she also went to great lengths in her efforts to assure the presence and availability of the therapist by the way she dressed, spoke, and selected and presented her ideas. Helen's unbearable fear of object loss was the basis for her promiscuity. The starting point in understanding this fear begins where Helen chose to begin in treatment, following two abortions and experiencing the impulse to kill herself.

There were multiple determinants of Helen's impulses to kill herself. Fundamentally, she felt rage toward her parents which was unconsciously directed against herself–she was going to "leave herself" as she had felt left by her parents. The impulse to destroy herself was also mobilized as punishment for both the conscious guilt she felt about her abortions (i.e., she separated from her babies the way Helen felt her parents had separated from her), and the unconscious guilt stemming from her fantasized incestuous tie to her father. However, it was Helen's initial magical fantasy in her suicidal ideas which unveiled the basis of her impulses.

Helen imagined that she would rid herself of the pain of her life and enter into a state of bliss. It was as though she were saying to herself "I will join the good mother who is gone by going where she is." Consistent with wished-for union, all of Helen's sexual fantasies centered on the theme of union and connection. In addition, Helen had reversed her sexual practices because of intensifying anxiety of object loss. As the anonymity of the man receded and was replaced by identity in tandem to the continuity and presence of Helen's sense of identity in relationship without the "cloud" of depersonalization, she abruptly withdrew from all sexual contact. Therefore, *one of the purposes of her promiscuity was the attempt to establish a sense of connection without the threats of rejection, separation, or unbearable loss.*

Kestenberg (1971) tells us that "the phallic wish to penetrate or be penetrated seeks to restore organ-object unity with the mother or her successor, the father" (pp. 92-93). Consistent with the motives in her thoughts of using her body in suicide, Helen had earlier used her body in efforts to preserve a tie to mother by magnifying the pain of her umbilical hernia to assure her mother's presence, and by immersing herself in the world of incestuous fantasies. In repetition of her efforts to preserve the tie to her mother by magnifying the pain of her umbilical hernia, in the wake of Helen's contemplations of killing herself–which itself resurrected separation–she sought out her internist who referred Helen to me. Helen's mistakenly addressing me in the name of the internist, and later having the fantasy that I was her gynecologist were repetitions of the urgency to confirm object ties through the use of her body.

The analysis of Helen's first sexual fantasy where she had depicted herself as deformed and immobilized ("a little girl, my leg is deformed, I can't walk, and some man is rescuing me while we're having sex") revealed defensive and narcissistic reparative efforts. Being little was expressive of wishes to replace guilt feelings deriving from incestuous fantasy with innocence through association to infancy. Being deformed combined both punishment for her sense of guilt, and at the same time revealed the surface of her sense of defectiveness and inadequacy.

Helen's primary image of herself as inadequate was specific to the nature of her early tie to her mother. The narcissistic injuries sustained by traumatogenic preoccupations of feelings of inferiority of her body in comparison to the pictures of women in her father's magazines remained. In this context, Helen also suffered from parental failures in the necessary mirroring of early exhibitionistic needs which included "demands for attention, approval, and confirmatory echoing of (her) presence" (Kohut, 1971, p. 124).

Just as in childhood where her incestuous fantasies and masturbatory practices were compensatory efforts to effect parental mirroring *in absentia,* her promiscuity in adulthood repeated a continuation of experience in which Helen sought to experience both the longed-for confirmation of object ties and visions of her body self as desirable, wanted, and adequate. Thus, a second fundamental *purpose at work in Helen's promiscuity was the narcissistic compensatory effort to use sensual experience and enactments to consolidate her sense of identity and relieve the painful disturbances in her impairments in self-esteem regulation* (see Stolorow, 1979, p. 39).

The purposes at work in Helen's use of her body and others in her promiscuity, her quest to evoke a specific trait in her "refinding" process, and her archaic wish to restore a longed-for and enduring tie with her mother is reflected in one poem of several which Bergmann (1987, p. 259) has selected to define love:

> I encounter millions of bodies in my life;
> of these millions I desire some hundreds:
> but of these hundreds I love only one.
>
> –Barthes, 1978

NOTE

1. I have used the term "psychopathological promiscuity" as defining of sexual behavior or intercourse which includes three aspects: (1) Within the sociocultural context of its occurrence, the sexual behavior *appears manifestly* as indiscriminate or nonselective, and is significantly and atypically frequent; (2) unconsciously or consciously the experience is conflictual to the person, or is motivated at least in part by conflict; and/or the behavior is secondarily generative of conflict or disturbance (e.g., guilt reactions); and/or (3) the sexual behavior, as a manifestation of psychodevelopmental impairment or arrest, is in the service of efforts to maintain one's self-esteem, sense of identity, and/or psychic organization (see Reich, 1960; Stolorow & Lachmann, 1980), (e.g., the behavior perpetuates

problematic compensatory efforts at narcissistic enhancement followed by deflation, fragmentation, and intensified vulnerability to psychic distress). (For further questions on definition of "promiscuity" see Maria Bergmann, 1969; Greenwald, 1973; Herskovitz, 1969; Huber, 1969; Pauling, 1969).

REFERENCES

Barthes, R. (1978). *A lover's discourse*. New York: Hill & Wang.

Bergmann, M. S. (1987). *The anatomy of loving*. New York: Columbia University Press.

Bergmann, M. V. (1969). A psychoanalytic approach to the genesis of promiscuity. In G.D. Goldman and D. S. Milman (Eds.), *Modern woman: Her psychology and sexuality* (pp. 211-227). Springfield, IL: Charles C Thomas.

Brenner, C. (1982). *The mind in conflict*. New York: International Universities Press.

Bernstein, S. B. (1983). Treatment preparatory to psychoanalysis. *Journal of the American Psychoanalytic Association*, 11(1), 11-25.

Eissler, K. R. (1963). *Goethe: A psychoanalytic study 1775-1786*. Detroit, IL: Wayne University Press.

English, H. B., & English, A. C. (1958). *A comprehensive dictionary of psychological and psychoanalytical terms*. New York: Longmans, Green.

Freud, A. (1965). *Normality and pathology in childhood*. New York: International Universities Press.

Freud, A. (1967). Comments on psychic trauma. *The writings of Anna Freud*. (Vol. 5, 221-241). New York: International Universities Press.

Freud, S. (1961). Three essays on the theory of sexuality. In J. Strachey (Ed. and Trans.), *The standard edition of the complete psychological works of Sigmund Freud* (Vol. 7). London: Hogarth Press. (Original work published 1905).

Freud, S. (1961). The infantile genital organization. In J. Strachey (Ed. and Trans.), *The standard edition of the complete psychological works of Sigmund Freud* (Vol. 19). London: Hogarth Press. (Original work published 1923).

Freud, S. (1961). Libidinal Types. In J. Strachey (Ed. and Trans.), *The standard edition of the complete psychological works of Sigmund Freud* (Vol. 21). London: Hogarth Press. (Original work published 1931).

Greenwald, H. (1973). Definition and treatment of female promiscuity. In D. S. Milman and G. D. Goldman (Eds.), *The neurosis of our time: Acting-out* (pp. 137-146). Springfield, IL: Charles C Thomas.

Herskovitz, H. H. (1969). A psychodynamic view of sexual promiscuity. In O. Pollak and A. S. Friedman (Eds.), *Family dynamics and female sexual delinquency* (pp. 89-98). Palo Alto, CA: Science and Behavior Books.

Huber, J. T. (1969). Discussion (of promiscuity). In G. D. Goldman and D. S. Milman (Eds.), *Modern woman: Her psychology and sexuality* (pp. 234-241). Springfield, IL: Charles C. Thomas.

Kestenberg, J. S. (1971). From organ-object imagery to self and object representations. In J. B. McDevitt and C. F. Settlage (Eds.), *Separation individuation: Essays in honor of Margaret S. Mahler* (pp. 75-99). New York: International Universities Press.

Kohut, H. (1971). *The analysis of the self.* New York: International Universities Press.

Lichtenstein, H. (1964). The role of narcissism in the emergence and maintenance of a primary identity. *International Journal of Psycho-Analysis, 45,* 49-56.

Pauling, F. J. (1969). Discussion (of promiscuity). In G. D. Goldman and D. S. Milman (Eds.), *Modern woman: Her psychology and sexuality* (pp. 241-245). Springfield, IL: Charles C. Thomas.

Reich, A. (1960). Pathological forms of self-esteem regulation. *The Psychoanalytic Study of the Child,* (15), 215-232.

Rothstein, A. (1986, September). *Special problems of preparation and "Opening Phase" activities with reluctant prospective analysands.* Paper presented at the Fall meeting of the American Psychoanalytic Association, New York City.

Stolorow, R. D. (1979). Psychosexuality and the representational world. *International Journal of Psycho-Analysis,* 60, 39-45.

Stolorow, R. D., & Lachmann, F. (1980). *Psychoanalysis of developmental arrests: Theory and treatment.* New York: International Universities Press.

Waelder, R. (1930). The principle of multiple function. Observations on overdetermination. In S. A. Guttman (Ed.). *Psychoanalysis: Observation, theory application* (pp. 68-83). New York: International Universities Press.

Webster, A. M. (1968). *Webster's seventh new collegiate dictionary.* Springfield, MA: G. & C. Merriam.

The Bubble

Charles Ansell

SUMMARY. The clinical concept of addiction, long associated with drug and chemical dependency, is here extended to emotional addictions. The subject of this chapter is addicted to "falling in love," which he significantly calls his "bubble." The dynamics of drug or chemical addiction in its intolerable need for a "fix," and the lows and highs which the subject feels before and after the craving is met, is here repeated in Ralph's need to "fall in love." Like the drug addict, the subject here is likewise indifferent to the social upheavals his addiction causes those near to him. The chapter portrays the early life of the subject as a critical determinant in his craving for an endless series of love relationships.

BACKGROUND

If there is a characteristic mood that weighs on Ralph, it would be distraught. I have never seen him at peace. Of course I have not seen him outside of my consultation room and though it should come as no surprise that some patients are understandably distraught at some sessions, Ralph is an exception. He is distraught at every session.

I recall our first session, now almost 20 years ago. He stood most

---

Charles Ansell earned his doctorate in psychology at Columbia University, followed by training in psychoanalysis at the National Psychological Association for Psychoanalysis. In private practice in California since 1960, he has been President of the California State Psychological Association and Editor of its publication for many years. He is currently on the faculty of the Cambridge Graduate School of Psychology in Los Angeles and is the author of numerous articles and book chapters on psychological themes.

Mailing address: Charles Ansell, EdD, 3815 Woodcliff Road, Sherman Oaks, CA 91403.

of the time. He paced the floor, flushed with an anxiety that fairly spilled out of every pore.

"I'm bored with life! It's the bubble that's killing me. I'm very romantic, too romantic. It's important to be in love. I've been married three times. Each one began with great romantic feelings, but marriage spoils it. Then I fall into a depression. I need to stay in love! When I'm not in love, I feel terrible."

Ralph married when he was barely 20 years old. The marriage lasted a year. For several years after that he rushed in and out of a half-dozen courtships. Each followed a predictable course and each came to the same end. It began at the discovery of a beautiful face that quickly engulfed him. The vision of the new lady haunted him endlessly. He could neither eat nor sleep. There followed the frenetic campaign of courtship, flowers by mail, gifts, phone calls, dinner dates. When the lady at last succumbed there followed weeks of ardent attention, then, mysteriously, the vision faded, followed by the inevitable depression. His post-love depressions settled over him much like the aura the epileptic feels at the onset of a seizure. This tortured state drove him at last to a therapist where he pleaded frantically to be lifted out of his agitated depression.

The mystery of the bubble haunted him. The "bubble" is Ralph's own felicitous term for his cyclic falling in and out of love. None of his bubble romances were either permanent or durable. It soon appeared that he had designed his bubble to lack both permanence and durability.

When he was 27 he fell in love again, this time with a woman he would later marry. His new wife had been divorced years earlier and had a daughter who lived in another state. That marriage produced a son within the year. Nine years after this marriage, his wife's daughter, a young woman he had never seen, came to visit. Once more, he was stricken. At the sight of the daughter, some 15 years younger than he, the bubble appeared again. Within a year he divorced his wife and married her daughter with whom he had a daughter. Three years later he separated from his wife, his former stepdaughter. A newer vision of loveliness had cut across his path and the bubble descended on him once again. It was this latter event that brought him to my attention.

I have often thought that when Kierkegaard wrote "Life must be lived forwards, but can only be understood backwards'' he foreshadowed a psychological view that would not come into currency until long after his death. But the task of understanding a life backwards is not simple. The events of our lives seem like a series of disparate, disconnected experiences. The challenge to group these clusters of experience into a pattern seems gratuitous, for no law compels history to obey patterns. Pattern makers are psychology's theorists, not law givers.

Ralph's bubble may be understood in part by an overpowering intensity he feels when the cycle of falling in love begins. Hence his plea to his therapist to lower the intensity. Failing to master the intensity, he falls victim to a compulsion.

The concept of addiction has lately entered the language of psychopathology to describe a far wider group of mental states than the popular chemical dependencies, as in drugs or alcohol. It now includes more complex behavioral disorders. Classically, addiction is said to exist when one's tolerance level for substances (drugs, alcohol) continues to rise so that the addict needs more and more before his tolerance level is reached. Loosely considered, Ralph is a love addict. His ''depressions'' are as much withdrawal pains as those the drug and alcohol addict suffers in withdrawal. Question: How can we pattern Ralph's earlier life's experiences to lead us to an understanding of his addiction? How can we explain his abnormal hunger for love?

He was an only child of a couple that would divorce when he was five. His mother remarried within the year of her divorce. Here are Ralph's memories of his mother:

''She was a beauty queen. She won a beauty contest, but she was very controlling and very overprotective. I never felt close to her. I never felt love from her or for her. But she was very seductive. I could manipulate her. She just wasn't up front with me, if you know what I mean.''

Ralph speaks of his father: ''He was a professional gambler. He would take people's bets on everything. He was arrested for taking bets. He opened a restaurant once. It didn't last long. I used to be scared of my father. He had a violent temper, but he never hit me.''

Of his childhood: ''When I was 3 or 4 years old I was the center of attention, but after my father left the house, I think it was about that time, I got fat. I mean, I got fat when I was 8 or 9. Kids made fun of me. I had oral sex with a cousin of mine until I was 16 or 17 years old."

Ralph on his present life: "With all my rushing to women, I've been impotent since I left my wife. I got real problems with my son. We just can't communicate. He's stubborn, demanding."

His "secret" life: "My most intense sex is watching my wife 'making it' with another man. I love to gamble. About every month I run to Las Vegas and gamble. I sit at poker sessions where the bets run into thousands. I go crazy there!"

On the surface a common thread seems to run through Ralph's love/sex life and his zeal for gambling. Both are insatiable, both drive him, and both are addictions.

When he speaks of his passion for his special kind of love/sex and for his compulsion to gamble, he acknowledges that he is out of control. He is, curiously, a financially successful business man. He has a sharp eye for the "buck." His business, retailing expensive merchandise, unlike more stable businesses such as manufacturing, requires him to be as much on top of his market as stock brokers are in following the daily ups and downs of stocks and bonds. Occasionally he will reach out to acquire small businesses out of his realm of experience mainly with a view to unload it, when it is profitable, or to close it when it is a loss. His business acumen includes a great deal of the professional gambler's outlook. Thus something of his pathology in his sex/love life and in his gambling seems reflected in his way of doing business.

He recognizes his difficulties in dealing with his wife and his son, and most recently with his daughter, the child of his third marriage. His complaints against his children seem familiar: "They've got to listen to me. I'm their father." (Read, "They should be under my control," reminiscent of his own complaint against his mother for controlling him in his childhood.)

CLINICAL EXPLANATIONS (PATTERN MAKING)

Perhaps the poet or the inspired essayist may proclaim that we are born anew each day, but memory, persistent, continuous memories (though some may seem to be "forgotten") remain alive to recall. We are all haunted by our yesterdays, for we are in great part the sum of all our yesterdays. A successful therapy that liberates us from the shackles of crippling yesterdays does not erase history; it repatterns our history to help us to understand and to forgive our past. Theodor Reik once said, "We must forgive our past if we are to have a future." And so I return to Ralph's past in this search for patterns.

To be sure, I will be relating cause to effect because I cannot believe that our lives are a series of random events. Connections must be made. There are those who may disagree with my judgment of what is to be connected, but it will not be a disagreement over the need to connect our life's events to character formation. Dissenters from my judgment may interpret causes differently, but I suspect we will all arrive at the same conclusions.

And now to my judgments.

Ralph's mother, we have learned, was a self-centered woman, concerned with her attractiveness. Ralph has told us that he was the center of attention when he was 3 years old. It seems plausible to suggest that his mother presented him as her creation, lauded his good looks. But even at 3 years of age he was left to feel used, exploited for her vanity. What lasting perspectives toward others, women particularly, was little Ralph left to grow on? When he learned, as children can learn painfully, that her "heart wasn't in it," that he was a toy to be played with, to be put on display, he may have felt frightened, certainly confused about his place in her life.

At every stage in Ralph's early development, from birth to adolescence he was shaken at the earliest foundations of character formation. As a consequence he grew in accordance with Erik Erikson's (1950) patterns. Mistrust grew instead of trust; shame and doubt grew in place of autonomy; guilt replaced initiative. When he needed assurances of his gender identity, his father loomed as a shadowy figure, remembered only for his violent temper, and remembered too for his father's arrest for criminal conduct. When he was barely five his parents divorced, leaving him to feel that his presence in their lives seemed of no consequence in their willingness to leave him out of their considerations. And when his mother married another man when Ralph was barely six, there were veiled references to memories of his mother entertaining men friends while he lay asleep in a nearby room.

He was led to early sexual precocity with a cousin. Indeed, he welcomed an early erotomania as a substitute gratification for the intimacy denied him by withholding parents. He fixated on hedonism early on.

Fixation is an interesting phenomenon. It suggests an over-determined outcome in Ralph's search for pleasure that had to be both sensual and immediate. Sensuality possessed him with such force that it "forced" him into newer and newer relationships throughout his later years. It shaped his preferences in sexual objects and it influenced him in his way of relating to others. A fixation, therefore, is more than a stopping-off place. It is a pervasive phenomenon that seeps through one's world outlook and attaches itself to the pursuits one chooses.

The social character of fixation is generally seen in its failure to enter a loving relationship at a level of maturity that insures the ability to live through crises and conflicts that invariably occur over time in the lives of men and women in marriage. Ralph's value system was rooted in an early life strategy that sought quick conquests to gratify the drive for the release of those tensions that afflict the immature. To put it simply, like the drug addict, Ralph needed quick fixes. He could not abide delays. No small wonder that over time the consequences of his need for a quick fix left a path of broken relations with all its attendant recriminations and rationalizations. This frightened him, but for him, therapy was still another quick fix. That too had to give him instant relief. This is the sad nature of fixations. It too often trips us up as we go on repeating one folly after another.

We must confront still another phenomenon long known to psychology: the curious way humans have of identifying with those who aggress upon them. Identification with the aggressor is by now the melancholy explanation of self-hatred among humiliated minorities. A humbled and abused member of a minority group turns on his own kind to oppress in imitation of the dominant group's attitudes toward him. Just as Ralph's mother was vain and narcissistic, demanding to be the center of attention, Ralph could in turn recall that at 3 years of age he was the center of attention. The recollection of occupying center stage seems now to be more a "screened memory," than historical reality. A child's strongly held wish becomes a later truth. Ralph is here identifying with the aggressor, his vain mother whose failure to attend him cast her as the "bad mother" but with whose narcissistic qualities he now identifies in his demands for the same instant gratifications (obedience) from the world under his control.

The depression which he complained about may not conform to the characteristics of a classical depression. Clinical depression is complex and there are many explanations at hand largely because the term itself is often misused or misapplied. Ralph's depression was more likely a panic state, for to be out of reach of someone to love, someone who could restore the "bubble," dropped him into an agitated state of despair. His agitation was genuinely felt, but it is closer to the child's fright at finding himself suddenly lost and forgotten. It is not a depression. The feelings that flood us at moments of crisis often reflect our level of maturity. The hysterical agitation which Ralph feels is continuous with his early life origins. The more mature have presumably learned to tolerate delay, but not Ralph. Delay for him evoked dark fears of abandonment.

A mature person, one who can at least tolerate delay, can recognize that a psychological problem may require weeks, perhaps months of patience during psychotherapy. Ralph is unable to sit through a series of scheduled sessions. He appears periodically at the crest of a crisis and despite his agreement that unraveling the mystery of his bubble may take more than one hour, he rarely returned for a follow-up session. In consequence, I have pieced his story together after some 10 years of periodic appeals for help.

It is significant that at the end of each session he stands above the therapist and draws out a wad of bills from which he peels off the fee for the hour. The transaction has the quality of a purchase made quickly at a convenience store. This may well be Ralph's less-than-conscious assurance to himself that he is not beholden to the doctor by agreeing to return for other sessions since control over his life would then pass to the doctor, a fate he has long feared. Or it might well mean his less-than-conscious reluctance to surrender the bubble.

An early alarm system set deep in his consciousness threatens him with a fear of annihilation if he should ever surrender the bubble. It is an illusion that has sustained him over the years. This has become an ecstasy worth the price of later suffering. Losing control, therefore, is dangerous because it can spoil the fantasy of childish omnipotence.

Consider his gambling. Psychologists are in general agreement that the compulsive gambler is guided by another kind of bubble, the fantasy of being possessed of certain magical powers. The gambler is driven by the need to conquer "Lady Luck" for to win her favor is to be the chosen one. Thus, paying the doctor on his terms is continuous with the fantasy of omnipotence. Ralph seems to say, "Doctor, I'll talk to you on my terms, only when I decide to call you. Your asking me to come in next week makes me a loser."

Living by a commitment to another person, a wife, or a child is "giving away the store." When Ralph reconciles with his wife after a bitter argument and after he had made angry threats of quitting the marriage, his wife has somehow learned to persuade him that he has been a naughty child, that he needs to come home to a good mother who loves him. He then pouts his grievances against her: She does not give sex willingly, she balks at his wish for three-way sex. Somehow, out of this morbid play Ralph becomes the child but yet retains control by demanding concessions that are clearly understood to be his personal conditions before peace is restored.

He rants against his son and his daughter because they are not obedient, they lack the respect due to a father. His complaints against his children are stated in moral maxims. His son does not attend to his work; his daughter, much younger than her half-brother, is too young to date (at 16).

I have met both children, separately, at their father's demand. Each of them was amused at their father's display of paternal concerns. Each of the children–the daughter at 16; the son at 28, now married and the father of an infant child–seems to say that each found their father hollow, if not foolish. Their father was the naked emperor who never wore regal garments. Ralph was never seen more "real" than when his children spoke of him and of the place he held in their lives.

Ralph's mercurial temperament, alternating between the highs of some intense love affair and the lows in the aftermath of despair at the end of the affair, places him among the manic-depressive types. But here, understanding mania or depression as Ralph experiences it, it takes on the character and coloration suggested in earlier references to the infantile base of most of his emotional life.

Overall, the picture that emerges in the foregoing explanation of Ralph's development through life, from a child of three to a man of 53, suggests an early-placed character formation that led him on a path in which he seemed to remain condemned–as Santayana put it–to repeat the past. If we fail to learn from the past, Santayana wrote, then we are compelled to repeat it.

More enlightened or more mature people finding themselves at a given moment in their lives stranded on familiar ground, a ground that has held them captive to a past frozen in glacial moorings, know that they must free themselves of past choices if they are to move forward. Those who break away from repetitive behavior learn to view life differently. These enlightened ones struggle against the lures of returning to the dubious comfort of a past that held them in bondage. But those who dared not move away from long-held repetitive life patterns face again and again the inevitable frustrations that Ralph met at the end of each bubble that burst. Addicts know the anguish that waits them after the momentary pleasure is gone. In drug dependency, the need is specific, the ecstasy is familiar, but the aftermath of craving grows even more powerful. They soon need another fix.

Clearly, what we are witnessing here is the complete loss of will. But are we comparing Ralph's bubble with the drug-dependent addict? The one is a chemical dependency and the other is a memory dependency. Ralph's memory of the anguish of an early emotional abandonment left him with a residue of hysteria that led him to follow a cyclical, repetitive life pattern. The world existed to provide him with instant gratification at his pleasure.

Were we to translate Ralph's thought and behavior into moral terms we would speak of him as selfish, inconsiderate, even antisocial. Suppose Ralph with his assorted traits grew up in a society whose traditions and belief systems did not permit the kind of acting out behavior that Ralph actually followed. To illustrate: The Ralphs of our Puritan ancestors might have turned their frustrations inward, but they might have expressed their frustrations by tyrannizing their environment with demands that those who stray should suffer banishment. Wasn't this in effect what Ralph did in his demand for obedience from his wife and children? Our Western literature is rich with stories of bitter men and women who directed their frustrations against others behind the mask of righteous Christian or Judaic or Islamic conduct. Today, when we set about to judge the obsessive moralisms of puritanism we turn to such terms as harsh, cruel, punitive.

RALPH: A MIRROR OF OUR TIME

Ralph alive and well in this last decade of the century is a modern man. His amoral behavior–selfish and inconsiderate–may be quite consistent for this period of our social history. He lived in accordance with an unspoken acceptance of permissible conduct for his time. The men in Ralph's world, hearing of his exploits, might be far more amused at his frolics than critical of his amoral behavior. We are not taught to add a moral dimension to the type of behavior described here. When I ventured to characterize his conduct as selfish, inconsiderate, and so on, I thought of the great number of public figures in public and private life who are continually exposed for scandalous conduct. Five United States senators were under investigation for accepting substantial contributions from an unscrupulous banker whose operations were in clear violation of the law. The banker paid the senators to intervene with the government on his behalf to spare him from prosecution. The banker had misled his investors, ordinary men and women, retirees, who purchased stock in his bank only to find the bank fail, leaving them to suffer great personal loss. The United States Government is obliged to protect the bank's depositors at a cost of two billion dollars.

There are investigations in the loss of millions of dollars in the government's housing program, money that was siphoned off by appointed officials for their personal gain. Judges accepted money from litigants to buy favorable verdicts for their benefactor. Financiers have been indicted for defrauding investors. Manufacturers are accused of adulterating medicines, baby foods, ordinary grocery items. Health providers have misrepresented claims of service offered to the public and have grown wealthy illegally.

Have we ventured far afield in comparing the amoral nature of Ralph's aberrant behavior with the bribes, thefts, and unlawful behavior of men and women in high places? We have grown accustomed to the endless series of exposures of unlawful conduct, and we have grown inured against the shock of surprise. We have cultivated a cynical veneer, an amused shrug of the shoulders and a wave of the hand, saying, "So what else is new?"

At its root, the unlawful behavior of public figures is in each case as amoral as Ralph's lamentable behavior driven by his addiction. There are of course certain differences between Ralph's pathology and the immoral acts of our public leaders. But there are also certain similarities. Ralph craved immediate gratification for his bubble. Public figures are more deliberate. They plan their strategies to achieve gratification at a later date. They simply take more time and effort to conceal their behavior from public view. At root also is the value of power. The senators exerted power over the bank regulator. Judges mete out justice to those who pay for his power to judge. Others add to their wealth for the power that wealth endows.

Ralph sought therapy at a time when his discomfort with the bubble grew acute. That discomfort suggests a growing awareness that something in his life seemed to be going awry. He had begun to protest against his imprisonment to a past that afflicted him with its compulsion to repeat his follies. It was as if Ralph was awakening to a view that he had best change if he wanted to find peace of mind.

To restate his predicament in loftier terms, Ralph had begun to feel remorse. When he cried out, "I'm bored with life," he could not know that he had chosen an apt term, for boredom is not listlessness, nor is it lethargy; it is a signal that something repressed yearns to be free. Boredom, far from plaguing us with a numbness of spirit, is acute agitation, not ennui. It is active, and often frightening in its chill of uncertainty.

And here lies a critical difference between Ralph's amoral behavior and the men and women in high places. Public figures are, if nothing else, sophisticated in the ways of the world. The common wisdom shrugs off another scandal with "His trouble is, he just got caught." Translated, that well-established wisdom means that the culprits were not guilty of criminal behavior. In our indifference to fresh news of still another exposure of misfeasance in office we dismiss it with the bitter "That's the way of the world . . . They're all the same, you know. Hey, that's politics." Or we have been known to say, "That's business as usual."

There may be some who, hearing Ralph's descriptions of his way of running between one bubble after another, would declare it sinful and would lead him to view the moral significance of his behavior. That approach indeed might be effective if Ralph were persuaded to enter onto a religious life in which he would learn to believe that change was a demand made on him by his God. But that task lies outside the realm of clinical psychotherapy. Clinical psychotherapy would not circumvent the task of helping Ralph to know and to understand his past, if he is to free himself from the ties that bind him to it.

Is there nevertheless a moral component implicit in the psychological task of uncovering a destructive past? Every successful psychotherapy is as much an experience in moral re-direction as it is a psychological exploration.

The prospect of persuading the sophisticated population of national leaders of the immorality in illegal behavior is remote indeed for we ourselves as private citizens are not alarmed at their behavior. We are far more alarmed at an elected official who differs from our beliefs; but stealing, bribing, lying–these offer us our amusement. Our national leaders cannot surprise us or disappoint us because we too know and expect the next scandal. We are by now immune against moral outrage at crime in high places.

We quickly agree that given Ralph's bizarre behavior in chasing his bubbles, he requires clinical attention, not only to save him from the pain of addiction, but to spare those others close to him from the damage that must follow from accommodating to his needs. It is when we view Ralph's behavior through a moral lens that our terms of discourse turn toward the language of the moralist. Ralph is indeed selfish and inconsiderate. Yet, within the language of the moralist, we fail to view the damage to public confidence when elected or appointed officials commit illegal acts bordering on the criminal. We judge them differently, if indeed we judge them at all.

A morally oriented society would take as its first responsibility the protection of the weak against the strong. The rampant abuse of children, whether at the hand of the child molester, or of the elected official who opposes child health measures, share in the same cruelty. The difference lies merely in the matter of the near and the distant. The child molester is near at hand to his victim. The legislator who denies children funds for health care stands at a distance from the child he or she deprives.

Human relations in all societies seem to stand on unequal footings: parent and child, teacher and student, employer and worker, government and citizen. All human pain in different measure rises out of the inequality in these relationships. If morality is to be observed in practice, we would then be vigilant in our protection of the weak from the undue exercise of power of the strong.

It may seem that I have gone far afield in these moral considerations but it would be a grave error to isolate the Ralphs of our society by denying that his choices mirror our time in history. Ralph is of our time; his disorder led him to choices in keeping with the moral practices of our time. Our national leaders in all of the major fields of our political and economic life are likewise acting in keeping with the moral practices of our time.

Investigators in the sorry field of child abuse have learned to broaden the range of child abuse beyond the clear and simple acts of physical cruelty onto the more lethal acts of neglect, physical and emotional. And Ralph was by any definition, abused as a child. It would be error to view Ralph from the wrong end of the telescope.

REFERENCE

Erikson, E. (1950). *Childhood and society*. New York: W.W. Norton.

Introducing Confusion to Create Change

Derek W. Paar

SUMMARY. The importance of confusion to the therapeutic process is examined. A 31-year-old female law student who has regularly had sex with strangers and no sex with her husband responds in a confused manner to a story which attempted to capture her life's dilemma. The change of behavior resulting from that confusion is explored with reference to two ideas: Knowing is no-ing, and confusion precedes creation.

She looks like an elegant eagle. A swirling wind and she glides on it. Moving clouds cover her for a bit until she rolls out from behind them. Always scanning with eyes that move in a still head. Scanning for prey. Swooping down from her glide she surrounds her meal and devours it at a ferocious speed. Squeezing life from the living she moves on through the sky scanning as she glides.

Liza gracefully moved a tiny bit further with each step than one would expect for a woman of her size. Not too much difference–2'9" for others became 3' for her. She moved with a flowing assurance. The few steps required to move from the hallway into my office and onto the awaiting chair were accomplished with a smooth ease, theatrical hands, and steady eye. She spoke with a kind of New England arrogance: a 25-letter alphabet, absent "R," and a sort of breathiness. Her hair was fashionably on the short side and framed a very attractive face with brown eyes gazing with scrutiny from behind wire-rimmed glasses. She swooped, glided, shook

Derek W. Paar, PhD, is Associate Professor in the Psychology Department, Springfield College.

Correspondence regarding this article should be sent to Derek W. Paar, Dept. of Psychology, Springfield College, Springfield, MA 01108.

hands, sat down, crossed her legs, tossed her head back, smiled, and said that she was becoming troubled with law school.

Liza was a 31-year-old second-year law student, wife, stepmother, and deliverer of sex to the unsuspecting. She first contacted the counseling center of the university where I worked because she felt rather tense about her life as a student as papers piled up and exams approached. Though she received very good grades, she expressed a real fear that her success was fraudulent and would soon be discovered. This complaint was really very common among her fellow law students, many of whom were my clients.

After the introductions and hello's, Liza told her tale. She had attended law school at age 30 at the behest of her husband, a lawyer and entrepreneur (a terribly haughty-sounding word anyway, but haughty in the extreme when pronounced with no "R"). She had recently been graduated from a very prestigious ivy league college. Prior to that she had been a student at a decently respected large urban university. Prior to that she had been a hairdresser in New Jersey married to a carpenter and hoping to save enough money to one day buy a house in the neighborhood that both Pete Seeger and John Cougar Mellencamp have sung about. Blue collar, unsophisticated, uncomplicated, bread over Bach, beer over burgundy, and hot dogs and beans over haute cuisine. The vaguely uncomfortable feeling welling within her was easily dismissed in the youthful exuberance of a growing life of suburban expectations.

She had been quite an ugly child. Gawky and gangly, features too large, eyes too weak, and trouble hearing all gave rise to monstrous teasing from brothers and sisters and peers; terribly accurate eyes always searching for what could be seen and not heard; and a refined style of speech more commonly encountered on Beacon Hill or in Harvard Yard than in the refineries along the Jersey Turnpike. In adulthood each and every one of these perceived deficits would be re-tooled under the careful tutelage of her own Henry Higgins–her first extramarital affair and presently her second husband.

This man of means was about 15 years her senior, a graduate of the university from which Liza's speech had its flavor, a mover and shaker, maker of money, father of two, and lawyer. Once these two collided he began the task of creating a female version of himself. She would quit hairdressing, enter college, and be his student of living. She too would be a lawyer, mover and shaker, mother of two, and sophisticate.

Liza finished 2 years at that large urban university before enrolling at the college with ivy over brick. Henry greased the skids to ensure her admission. Liza never really knew if she was acceptable on her own. With Henry's help that would never be an issue. It most surely had not been an issue at her first college as the intelligence she naturally possessed became secondary to the well-cultivated intelligence owned by her husband. He generated the ideas, he wrote the papers, and he pressed her on to the ivy prize. That press continued through that institution and on to law school.

The pleasure she felt at her new life took center stage for a few years and one day was replaced by its understudy–resentment that her life was not her own. This resentment swelled her attraction for other men. First just a glance which was held a wee bit longer than convention would say is appropriate. Then a quick encounter with known and familiar men. Soon complete strangers became her best friends for a few minutes. Visits to service stations became experiences that 50 years from now old men will need to remind themselves really occurred. A pimplyfaced kid, voice cracking, and eyes and pants bulging, was told to, "fill it up." A service was duly provided in some greasy hidden spot in Shell, Exxon, Mobil, and generic gas stations all across Southern New England. Blemished faces cleared and resentment was drained away. Liza pursued, pleasured, left, and returned home to Henry's house with a salt-water front yard and two overbearingly wealthy adolescents 13 and 14 years her junior. Instant motherhood and misery awaited her as one stepdaughter lamely tried to kill herself and the other one whined on. Henry gave Liza the kids while he busied himself with more important things.

Liza's initial account of her marriage bordered on the ideal. She and Henry never argued nor shared a cross word. The fact that they went months between sexual encounters with each other seemed to be no problem to her when held in comparison to the lack of discord. This asexual nature of the marriage was due, as she saw it, to the age of her spouse.

Talk of law-school problems quickly stopped as her conversation took a more personal path. She was in a life which did not fit. It was assigned to her and carried out for her by a person whom she loved and hated, needed and resented, wanted to squeeze and strangle. Trying to capture the unspoken, but oozingly evident resentment in her life, I spent the last half of one of our hours together relating a story which had recently occurred to me but which I attributed to a friend in Idaho.

THE STORY

A friend of mine from graduate school lives in southeast Idaho near Pocatello. His parents, after years of struggling, finally were able to afford something they had long dreamed of. They bought a house on Bear Lake. What a big, beautiful, clean, deep, attractive lake! Eagles fly and deer roam. Such a pleasant place to spend time. Well, my friend's parents shortly had another chance they had only dreamed about–they got to visit Europe for a few months last fall. Those new and exotic places they could only dream about at one time in their lives now became real to them. I mean, these were not rich people. Geez, it all seemed like a dream. It also seemed like a dream to my friend–he could now use the house on the lake whenever he desired. So, every Friday after work last fall he would come home around 5:00 or 5:30 and be all ready to grab his new wife and her daughter and hop in the car and drive the 2 or 3 hours over to the lake. God was he excited! What on earth could be better–surrounded by people he loved and who loved him back, a house on a lake, and time to unwind from a job that took a toll on him. And, without fail each and every Friday after work his wife would fail to be ready. Her child would never be adequately prepared–she would need more attending to and the stuff never got together in time to leave. And she always seemed to find something else to do. His thought was to just put some stuff in a bag and go. And each and every Friday they stayed home. And each and every Friday she promised to be ready early Saturday morning to travel. Each and every Saturday they ended up leaving at noon and arriving at 2:30 or 3:00. He and his stepdaughter made a mad dash to the lake to boat and fish and play. They did it by themselves because his wife stayed back in the house to tidy up. That night when the child was asleep he and his wife also played and had fun in a way that only adults could play and have fun. Well, that surely pleased both a great deal. Sunday arrived and when my friend and his stepdaughter again visited the lake to play, his wife and her mother remained in the house preparing for a big greasy stuffed chicken dinner. Now neither child nor husband wanted such stuff. They wanted to play longer and just grab a burger on the way home that night. No big deal. My friend's wife really didn't want to cook that damned bird and really hated the whole damned mess–all that cooking and cleaning up afterward. Each Sunday they sat down to eat very quietly. My friend and her child could never ever be grateful enough to please her. She hated cooking and cleaning and then hated that no one congratulated her on doing the very thing that she hated doing. They hated having to eat it. She hated having to make it. The ride home was always quiet. Both could feel that smoldering feeling in their gut toward the other for having done such a thing to the other. Geez, I see that our time is up. See you next Friday. Bye.

Liza left with the damnedest look on her face. It seemed to say, "Christ, what a waste of time." She returned with roughly the same look the following Friday and proceeded to take me apart. "I have been thinking about that ridiculous story you told me last week about the big greasy chicken dinner. I thought about it all week long. I thought about it all the time. What a stupid dumb story. I do not know what you meant. What a stupid assinine story. I have never heard such a stupid assinine story in my life. I have no idea what you meant. If this weren't free I'd just stop payment on the check. I thought about that stupid story all week long and I still do not know what you meant. It was stupid. I do not know what you meant. I couldn't stop thinking about it. I do not know what you meant . . ."

I replied, "So, how was your week?"

She countered, "Well, I saw my boyfriend after our session last week and broke up with him. He's been a real pain in the ass anyway. That evening I went home and had a loud and ferocious argument with my husband. You know we hadn't fought since last year. And, Saturday we spent in bed making love for the first time in months and months. And I still think that story was the stupidest most ridiculous thing I have ever heard in my life. I could not stop thinking about it. I do not know what you meant."

Consider these two thoughts before looking more closely at what transpired between me and my client: (1) knowing is no-ing; (2) confusion precedes creation.

KNOWING IS NO-ING

In a universe of infinite connectedness and motion the only possible way anything can be created is through the exclusion of other potential possibilities. In order to "know" anything we say "no" to all else. Physics in the 20th century (and for that matter chemistry, biology, and some areas within psychology) seems to be moving away from the notion of a particalized universe and moving more toward a vision of a universe of full and complete connection existing, at best, in some kind of strange order, or at worst (and perhaps most exciting and frightening), in no order at all (Bohm, 1983; Capra, 1984; Kelly, 1955; Meyers, 1984; Prigogine & Stengers, 1984). From this starting point of a confusing and connected universe with no inherently distinct features, where nothing *is* in and of itself, existence in the physical realm–objects–and existence in the personal realm–(feelings, thoughts, perceptions, actions . . . all of which we shall call) knowing–can only occur through the negation of all the rest of a universe save that which is known. We know only by no-ing. We can never ever completely know what something is, we can only know what it is not. We see only the edges and never the substance.

Mandlebrot (1977) writes of a "coastline so irregular and winding as to be much longer than the straightline distance. Various ways of evaluating it all lead to the conclusion that the final estimated length is not only extremely long but in fact so long that it is best considered infinite" (p. 27). When one follows all of the nooks (within nooks within nooks . . . not to even begin to mention all of the crannies within crannies . . .) of any coastline of any length, one begins to conclude that that coastline is truly without limit. In order for us to create some order and bring some sensibility to this venture we have to limit the infinite. We use some measuring device and walk it up the coastline. The unit of measure that we use determines what we can conclude (a notion more than vaguely reminiscent of Einstein's statement that nature is exposed to us in the ways we ask our questions). If we use a mile as a measure we will get one length, if we use a foot-long ruler we will get another length, if we use a caliper set at a centimeter we will find another length, and if we use a "Derek" (6' 1/2") we will reach quite another conclusion. An infinite area found between the first point on the measure and the terminal point on the mile, foot, centimeter, or "Derek" must all be ignored or else we would never be able to come to any knowledge. "No" must be said to all of that infinite area (both coast and measure) so that we may "know."

William James' (1890) well-used metaphor of the sculpture residing within the stone also captures this idea of existence through "no-ing." The sculpture (or thought, or feeling, etc.) appears only as non-sculpture (other thought, or other feeling, etc.) is chipped away. The object takes on life through the elimination of part of the larger block.

Surely the idea that "knowing is no-ing" is found in the work of Darwin. His master work can be (very, very briefly) summarized as saying that nature only determines what will not survive, not what will survive. Within that negation a virtual infinite variation may exist. And, as that negation continues on, as more and more metaphorical stone is chipped away, the life of the known becomes threatened. As a species becomes too specialized and lacking in diversity, the species may die. The recent serious decline in the cheetah population shows this need for difference within the limitation of the species.

Color (and sound and pain, etc.) comes to life in a process of no-ing. Within the infinite range of color we see blue through the exclusion of all other color. Within that negation of other potential color we may see blues of all hues from the shell of a robin's egg to the jackets worn by sailors in formal winter dress. When too much has been excluded, or when too much has been included, color ceases. Inclusion of all color produces white light. Exclusion of all color produces black.

I will stop beating the poor reader over the head with more evidence which supports the notion that knowledge is created by "no-ing." Suffice it to say that this principle is seen in brain functioning (Pribram, 1971), philosophy (Kuhn, 1962), math (Korzybsky, 1950), and on, and on. Knowing *is* no-ing. Liza knew her husband, lover, stepchildren, and life only by saying no to all other possible meanings.

CONFUSION PRECEDES CREATION

Confusion almost always is presented as something to run from, something to kill. Recent news reports of the impending change in Eastern Europe, Central America, and Asia all contain some scary and negative reference to the present chaos or confusion being experienced. Only occasionally has "confusion" been identified as a state or trait which has power and potential. It is my contention that confusion is *absolutely* a precondition to the creation of anything at all which is new.

Though rarely directly expressed as confusion, similar states and traits (novelty, uncertainty, etc.) have been mentioned by those who have studied creativity (Amabile, 1983; Gordon, 1974; Mansfield & Busse, 1981; Maslow, 1966; Wertheimer, 1959). All have expressed the idea that it is important to step away from the problem to construct a different and creative solution. In stepping away from the problem, a new set of possibilities is able to be explored. My belief is that, in stepping away, a sense of confusion may envelop the person from which newer and stranger limitations may grow. My belief is that confusion is much more prevalent and much more important than researchers and thinkers may have thought.

We humans have the knack of getting more confused than all other creatures on earth. We are born the physiological equivalents of fetuses and begin the (what seems to parents like an interminably) long period of exploration and nurturing. This helpless and confused condition is the single best thing we have in our favor in our struggle to fit. We surely are not the strongest, most sensorially acute, or the biggest. We do, however, have the unique advantage of being able to scratch our heads, look up into the sky, and say, "What the hell is going on here???"

Confusion (or at least a phrase expressing that sentiment) is found to be a critical element in the shift of thought one finds in science. In a Kuhnian (1962) philosophy of science the new paradigm arises from the ashes of confusion. When Feyeraband (1978) writes that "Without chaos no knowledge. Without frequent dismissal of reason, no progress" (p. 179) he is most assuredly calling our attention to the fact that confusion is the land of fertile fields. Even his frequent and friendly critic, Lakatos (1970), seems to agree with this thought in a softened and understated way in the expression of his belief that it is imperative to experience novelty in order for there to be a change in the way in which science perceives.

Certainly individual scientists exhibit this lost and floating sensation of confusion prior to the creation of any new conception of the universe. Einstein, Kepler, and Kekule (to name but three) had to experience a confusion before the creation of any new invention or thought. One can see this same sort of confusing process in something more common. Bronowski (1978) speaks of this when he writes that one chess player may be better than another not because she or he is more controlled and less prone to error. Quite the contrary, the better chess player "makes more mistakes, by which I mean more imaginative mistakes" (p. 110). He concludes that all imaginative inventions are errors when compared to the normal or usual.

On our more mundane human scale, far from art, science, philosophy, or even thoughtful games such as chess, confusion is also seen as utterly necessary for any new event, idea, thought, or action to occur. This is written with two pictures flowing in my head. One is of Michael Jordan and the other is of my 5-year-old daughter, Chelsea. While Michael Jordan can do the typical things one would expect on the basketball court, the atypical and astounding maneuvers he exhibits all occur when he is confused. Caught in mid-air, not knowing (no-ing) what will be, he creates magic with his body in the nick of time. Chelsea, not knowing (no-ing) as much as her father, produced an American flag and a necklace out of tape, bits of paper, and a strand of straw from a fireplace broom last night while we watched a basketball game. Her limitations are so loosely organized at age 5 that she is able to create new meaning for herself and great joy for me. Again, I will refrain from bruising the skull of the reader with more tub-thumping on the power and importance of confusion. I will finish with one last comment. Confusion is the ground from which new meaning may grow. Confusion is not knowing, or no-ing. Confusion precedes creation. Though Liza entered therapy frustrated and resentful she was never confused about her life. It existed in a well-ordered and well-limited way which excluded other possible ways.

Liza's frequent punitive lament, "I do not know what you mean,' takes on a different understanding when the word know is replaced by the word no. That phrase now becomes "I do not *no* what you meant." Her confusion was revealed as she was unable to establish any firm limitation (any knowing/no-ing) to the amorphous message which was delivered to her. This new nagging sense of a confusion which she experienced allowed/forced her to *create* new meaning.

EXAMINING THE INTERACTION

There was no specific behavior change I hoped would result from that story. I didn't care if she altered her relationship to her husband or lover. I really had no intended goal that she would reach with the introduction of that story. My single hope was that the story would somehow capture the spirit of her entrapment in a different and unpredictable way. My belief was that in order for the story to have a chance at power it had to be delivered with unloaded dice. By aiming at a specific target the strength of the story would fail. It would be too concerned about rightness and wrongness and would not allow Liza to actually play with the ideas herself.

The story of the big greasy chicken dinner had both a strange familiarity and a familiar strangeness to Liza. Though the story *was* strange to her, there was a subtle ring of familiarity to it as well. A story too strange would have been rejected (said no to) and would not have had any impact. Speaking about clams at the bottom of the

Chesapeake Bay (for example) would surely be strange to her but would more than likely be so strange as to be rejected very quickly. Those clams, no matter how appropriate, would likely fail to be incorporated into any part of *her* own personal "no-ing system" (her own sense of life). We may conclude that the story I told her was familiar enough to be invisible (so well no-ed as to be taken for granted) and yet strange enough that she could not categorize, limit, or know it (no it).

The story gave Liza the opportunity to experience a delicious sensation which had been out of her range of experience for some time–confusion. For the first time in a long time in her life with Henry she was able to scratch her head and ask, "What the hell is going on here?" Prior to that story she had a clean and well-defined limit, a certain no-ing, of her relationship to her husband, lover, and stepchildren. Those limits were as real to her as the law of gravity is to a falling apple. She saw no possibility that that limit was a personal fiction created and employed by her to make sense of a previously confusing situation.

In order for any new behavior, thought, feeling, or perception to become real, the previous no-ing system (behavior, thought, feeling, perception) must be killed. It is killed through the introduction of confusion. In this case confusion was provided in the form of a series of strange and familiar ideas which expanded to death the previous no-ing system she employed to know these segments of her life.

That expansion of a no-ing system to the point of death is one of two directions one may travel to achieve confusion. Both the inclusion of too much extraneous material (expansion of the no-ing system) and the exclusion of too much extraneous material (contraction of the no-ing system) can produce confusion. The same end of these two polar-opposite approaches can best be seen in systematic desensitization and flooding. Systematic desensitization introduces into a no-ing system a new difference–calm, for example–which then acts like a killer virus. This new and subtle difference worms its way into the no-ing system of object and panic and expands to the point of confusion the old limitation. Flooding achieves the end of fear in a contradictory way through the elimination of all possible escapes into extraneous thought or feeling. All become the same. This lack of difference and variation has the same effect on fear that lack of difference and variation has had on the cheetah population–demise and eventual extinction.

The birth of confusion produces no certificate of guarantee. No one can predict what path will be carved out of the forest of possibility. All one can be sure of is that some path, different from the previously well-worn one, will emerge. The path and meaning will be a personal creation. The new no-ing will be fluid in its birth and easily subject to change in the same way a child at birth is so easily altered by the whimsical moves of its parents. (Scientists in the new field of "chaos" have a term for this. They call it sensitive dependence on initial conditions.)

This article, in all probability, is not the correct vehicle to expound at length on what unites therapeutic approaches across the spectrum–from psychodynamic to cognitive to experiential to behavioral. I will simply leave the reader with this thought: Psychotherapy is about the killing of prior thoughts, feelings, and actions through the introduction of confusion which then allows for a play of different potential no-ings, which eventually settles down into more limited patterns of no-ing (thoughts, feelings, and actions). This process is present in shallow and deep therapies, rapid and prolonged therapies, and cannot be escaped. This process can be seen clearly in my encounter with Liza.

REFERENCES

Amabile, T. (1983). *The social psychology of creativity*. New York: Springer-Verlag.

Bohm, D. (1983). *Wholeness and the implicate order*. New York: Methuen.

Bronowski, J. (1978). *The origins of knowledge and imagination*. New Haven: Yale University Press.

Capra, F. (1984). *The tao of physics*. New York: Bantam New Age.

Feyeraband, P. (1978). *Against method*. New York: Schocken Books.

Gordon, W. J. J. (1974). Some source material in discovery by analogy. *Journal of Creative Behavior*, *8*(4), 239-257.

James, W. (1890). *The principles of psychology* (Vol. 1). New York: Holt.

Kelly, G. (1955). *The psychology of personal constructs*. New York: Norton.

Korzybsky, A. (1950). *Manhood of humanity*. Lakeville, CT: The International Non-Aristotelian Library Publishing Company.

Kuhn, T. (1962). *The structure of scientific revolutions*. Chicago: University of Chicago Press.

Lakatos, I. (Ed.). (1970). *Criticism and the growth of knowledge*. Cambridge: Cambridge University Press.

Mansfield, R. S., & Busse, T. V. (1981). *The psychology of creativity and discovery: Scientists and their work*. Chicago: Nelson Hall.

Maslow, A. (1966). *The psychology of science*. Chicago: Henery Regnery.

Meyers, N. (Ed.). (1984). *Gaia: An atlas of planet management*. Garden City, NY: Anchor.

Pribram, K. (1971). *Languages of the brain*. Englewood Cliffs, NJ: Prentice-Hall.

Prigogine, I., & Stengers, E. (1984). *Order out of chaos*. New York: Bantam.

Wertheimer, M. (1959). *Productive thinking*. New York: Harper and Brothers.

Career Promiscuity: Patients Who Cannot Commit to a Career

Linda B. Hopkins

SUMMARY. The author examines the problem of young adults in therapy who cannot make career choices and who suffer from identity diffusion. The problem is traced to parents who have not modeled healthy career choices and also to societal influences. The author presents a model for treatment wherein the therapist becomes a central figure in the repetitive patterns and helps the patient to act in a new way and make meaningful choices. Three illustrative cases are presented.

Above all, act impulsively: don't let yourself get stuck between alternatives, or you're lost. You're not that strong. If the alternatives are side by side, choose the one on the left; if they're consecutive in time, choose the earlier. If neither of these applies, choose the alternative whose name begins with the earlier letter of the alphabet. These are the principles of Sinistrality, Antecedence, and Alphabetical Priority–there are others, and they're arbitrary, but useful.

–John Barth, *The End of the Road*, p. 83

The book *The End of the Road* by John Barth (1969) describes a talented young man who is totally lost in life, with no significant

---

Linda B. Hopkins, PhD, is a clinical psychologist and psychoanalyst in private practice in Philadelphia. She is an instructor at the Philadelphia School of Psychoanalysis. Address correspondence to the author at 1521 Locust St., Ste. 600, Philadelphia, PA 19102.

relationships and no career. A psychiatrist finds him in a train station, sitting "frozen" because of his inability to decide where to go, given all the possibilities. The psychiatrist takes him into his care and helps him through "Reality Therapy" in which he is pressured to make choices and take action so that he can have an identity. The above quote is an example of the therapist's advice. This paper provides an alternative approach to patients who have the same problem. It is about young adults in therapy who have what I will call career promiscuity: They are unable to make commitments to a career which has meaning for them. They are people with a great deal of potential who never get beyond their potential. They may go from one career to another indiscriminately or they may stay with one career without making a true commitment. The paper will provide a theoretical explanation of the problem and give suggestions for psychotherapy, with illustrative case studies.

DESCRIPTION OF THE PROBLEM

Erik Erikson (1968), in his classic work on adolescent identity formation, provides a description of the centrality of career choice in consolidation of identity. In moving from identity crisis to identity resolution, the adolescent must first rebel from parents in order to become a separate person, and then return to accept selected parental values so that the career choice is not based solely on rebellion and so that the person can fit into the larger society. Commitment to a career comes before long-term commitment to a relationship, and the successful choice of a career actually sets the stage for successful choice of a partner.

Therapists see many patients who have not been able to make successful career choices. These are talented people, who often report having been told repeatedly, "You could do anything (or many different things) for a career." They may go from one career to the next or, as in the common case of people who cannot finish a PhD dissertation, they may stick with one career they cannot master. They live in poverty or are supported by their parents as they watch more and more of their college friends get established in life. They are repeatedly given the advice to "just choose" or "just finish" but this is rarely helpful. As they grow up from their 20s into their 30s, their families tend to become increasingly frustrated and concerned about them. The patients themselves become increasingly unhappy and at this point they often enter therapy.

Patients with career promiscuity come from families where the career of one or both of the parents has not been successful in some way. Often the father has had financial success, and the parents' financial support undermines the patient's motivation to choose a career. Adolescents who come from poorer families are more likely to show premature commitment to a career they hate because they can't afford career promiscuity. However, the successful father usually works too hard and is not happy. Thus the parents may give their children the message "Don't be like your father" but they do not provide an alternate example. Often the mother herself had been interested in the field that attracts the child, but she never pursued a career successfully, so the message is also "Don't be like your mother." In a common pattern, the children may go into the arts, rather than business, but this doesn't please the parents because the arts generally do not offer financial stability and these parents want the child to make a good income, like the father. The child, lacking role models, flounders.

To some extent, the problem of career promiscuity seems to reflect a national problem. In order to make a successful career choice, a person needs to have role models who demonstrate how to work successfully. Successful work means enjoying one's work and also setting limits on it so that one can enjoy other aspects of life. Yet a recent survey of Americans revealed that we "work far too much, never have enough time to spend with family or friends, have stress levels escalating to an all-time high and generally appear out of control" (survey by Priority Management described in *The Philadelphia Inquirer*, Cl, December 26, 1989). We all know many people who fit this description, people who work too hard and lose their enjoyment of life, or people who dislike their work but feel unable to shift careers to something they would enjoy more. In fact, when a successful person does make a major career shift the story is often reported in the newspaper. Very few children today grow up with parents who model for them a healthy work life. Girls may suffer even more from this since there is a relative lack of same-sex models for them–that is, grown women who can be mentors and also show them how to successfully combine work in the "masculine" world with the raising of children. However, boys and girls, women and men, all of us in today's world need more models of people who work successfully and who also feel spiritually nourished and nourishing. The financial situation of middle-class families has changed and families which used to survive on the salary of one parent now require that both parents work to maintain their standard of living. In this period of readjustment, people have a difficult time balancing all their different roles.

The national problem certainly relates to the development of career promiscuity. Still, most young adults are able to choose a vocation. This paper is about those who are stuck in the decision-making stage.

THEORETICAL UNDERSTANDING OF THE PROBLEM

This paper will approach the issue of career promiscuity from the point of view of object-relations theory and paradigmatic psychology (Nelson, Nelson, Sherman & Strean, 1968). We will go beyond the usual oedipal explanations, which explain career pathology as involving a lack of identification or a rivalry with the father, because we believe that the most basic problem is preoedipal. Certainly there are some patients with career problems that are basically oedipal and these patients can be helped with interpretations and understanding of the problem. However, we will be focusing on the difficult patients, who are "stuck" in therapy and in life, and who do not respond to interpretation and understanding alone. These difficult patients are seen as caught in a repetition compulsion which has its origins at an early age.

The world of work is the adult version of a child's play. The translation of childhood pleasure and amazement during play into adult work gives the work its meaningfulness. Hendrick (1943) writes that play is the child-equivalent of adult work. Padel (1987) gives Winnicott credit for the awareness of the centrality of play to adult life, stating "Winnicott's own greatest contribution to technique has been to get therapists to think of their own patients as people who in childhood or adolescence forgot or never developed the knowledge of how to play and who now need to play" (p. 135).

Our model of career promiscuity, or the inability to play well as an adult, is based on the work of Kubie (1963) and Nelson (1968). As a young child develops, she or he repeatedly cathects new experiences with distinct memory traces that can be positive or negative and can be helpful or harmful to development. This repeated cathexis goes along with a primary experience of being real, alive, and in contact with objects, even if the original memory trace is predominantly negative (Nelson, p. 30). If the feeling of being alive during times of play occurred in conjunction with pain of some type (e.g., shaming, disapproval, restraint, or scolding), then the child's later work behavior will be experienced as unpleasant and/or self-defeating. This theory explains the Freudian concept of repetition compulsion, wherein the person repeats the early childhood experiences, even if they were unpleasant.

The same model can be used to explain failure to establish successful object relationships, that is, failure in intimacy, in adulthood. However the choice of career has origins in a later period of childhood, since the play, per se, is not part of the earliest experiences of infancy. The father, or the absent father, is a central figure in the early play and later in career choice. Thus the career repetition may be less primitive and more open to modification than intimacy repetitions, even though both are preverbal or preoedipal in nature. This is why we find many examples of people who have successful careers but very disturbed object relations. The pattern of disturbed careers and successful object relations is less likely.

The theory of self psychology as developed by Kohut (1977) provides an explanation of career promiscuity which is totally compatible with the above model. Self psychology focuses more directly on the actual objects in the patient's early life. Pathology would be seen as developing through failure of the objects to mirror the early play experiences and/or failure to provide models for idealization and identification. Study of the parents of patients with career promiscuity provides examples of this type of failure of the objects, as will be shown in the case studies presented below.

THEORY OF THE THERAPY

Since the patients in this study have preoedipal pathology, we will assume that interpretation has little value. Interpretive psychotherapy could go on for years, with patient and therapist increasingly conscious of the origins of the problem, but with no substantive improvement. The change must come from the cathexis of feeling states, not from ideas (Nelson, 1968).

Although tripartite relationships are usually considered oedipal and dual relationships preoedipal, the model presented here is tripartite and preoedipal. The theory is that the patient is stuck in a particular fixed pattern of self-career-object pathology. The particular object involved in career pathology is always the father (or absent father) and often the mother also. Specific negative affective experiences are associated with this triad. For example, the patient may associate his or her work with memories of the father's lack of belief in the patient's potential, or the mother's overprotectiveness, or the parents' ambivalence toward their own careers. The dystonic affects associated with these memory traces interfere with the patient's career progress. If the relationship were a dual relationship, rather than tripartite, the patient would have a direct relationship to career and could make choices without the interference of negative affect. Thus a goal of therapy is to remove the patient's parents from their central position in the relationship to career. Prior to attainment of a dual relationship, however, the therapist must take the place of the parent and provide a new experience.

One of the greatest obstacles to successful therapy is the fact that the tie to the parents, even bad parents, is amazingly difficult to break. The task of the therapist is to become just as important as the parent, or more important. The means to this end is transference, wherein the patient experiences the therapist as a parent substitute and the affective charge is just as great as that to the parent. Meerloo and Nelson (1965) write that patients come to therapy with the transference "script" already written and with hope, as well as fear, that the therapist will play a central role. As Kohut (1979) has pointed out, transference is not simply a repeat of an earlier experience; the relationship to the therapist can develop into something new, which should have happened developmentally, and still retain the intensity of the repetitive experience. Thus in our model, the therapist aims to first become very important and then to become a new type of object. When the stalemate of the repetitive experience is resolved, change can occur.

There is no single model for the recommended type of relationship of patient to therapist, only that it be different from the relationship to the parent, equally intense, and in a direction toward greater openness to the outside world. It is generally essential that throughout the therapy the therapist present a model of enjoyment of his or her career, with commitment but not overcommitment. Sometimes in a successful therapy there will never be an intensive focus on the discussion of the career impasse; improvement regarding career occurs because the new object relationship helps the patient to become open to new patterns in the pursuit of a career. Once a talented person starts making a healthy commitment to a career, there is usually substantial reinforcement from the outside world, in the form of praise, financial gain, or recognized achievement. Furthermore, the patient experiences a rise in self-esteem which is reinforcing. The improvement in career status may come prior to improvement in object relations, for reasons discussed above.

CLINICAL ILLUSTRATIONS

In this section, I will present three case studies which illustrate the model of treatment for career promiscuity.

Mr. R.–An Emotionally Deprived Patient

Mr. R., a 29-year-old unmarried graduate student in American History, came to treatment with a female therapist complaining that he was "stuck" in a PhD program he could not finish because he was not sufficiently talented to finish his degree. He had a thesis topic and had written half of the thesis, but he did not believe he could finish. His advisor, a famous and busy man, did not provide much encouragement and refused to even read the thesis until it was in final form. The patient had exhausted his grant money and was working as a substitute teacher. Most of his peers had gotten their degrees and left town. Mr. R. was depressed, lonely, and exhausted and he had extremely low self-esteem. He asked the therapist to help him figure out what to do.

The patient came from a lower-middle-class family that had no understanding of the complexities of his field of specialization. Neither his parents nor his brother had gone to college. The father was an industrial worker who had retired on disability at age 50 for a bad back; the mother was a file clerk who hated her work; and the brother was an auto mechanic. The parents had a cold, distant relationship with each other and the father in particular was incapable of intimacy with anyone. The mother was emotionally close to her children but she was bossy and opinionated; whenever she was challenged she withdrew into self-pity. The brother was a fairly warm but limited man who had made a successful marriage.

The patient talked well and told the story of his life for the first year of treatment. However, he made no progress with his work and this was a major barrier to his happiness and potentially to the therapy, since his income was very low. The patient had a warm but somewhat "false" relationship with the therapist and the atmosphere of the treatment was positive but limited in intensity. Increasingly, both patient and therapist were growing impatient and discouraged about the patient's potential to obtain a PhD.

In one session, the therapist asked Mr. R to tell her exactly what he had written so far, in great detail. To her surprise, Mr. R had done high-quality original work which was very interesting. However, nobody had given him praise because nobody knew about it. The patient was repeating the familial pattern in which he was not known for himself and not appreciated. The therapist decided to take an active and encouraging stance toward the thesis, to see if the stalemate could be broken. She praised his work and asked him to tell her in detail every session what he could achieve the next week. She suggested that he keep his goals reasonable so that he would have success every week and every week she complimented him for keeping to his goals. Within 6 months, the patient finished his thesis, and even won a prize for his work. He got a job in his field and his standard of living and general state of mind were greatly improved. Three years later, he is still doing well at work but he has not yet found a woman to marry, even though he is impatient for marriage and children. The relationship with the therapist is now quite intense and it seems likely that the patient's unconscious agenda is the idealization of the therapist as the perfect mother/wife, making other candidates pale by comparison.

This patient is an example of someone who has been emotionally deprived early in life. He longed for objects who would reverse the pattern by showing interest in him but he did not stimulate interest in others because he hid his strengths from them. The therapist was surprised to discover his talents. When she praised and encouraged him, he accepted her involvement and the repetition was actually rather easy to break. In contrast to the career success, the repetitive pattern of relationships with people was more resistant to intervention.

Case No. 2–A Negatively Suggestible Patient

Ms. M., a 27-year-old unmarried graduate student in Economics, came to treatment with a female therapist complaining of depression and problems in finding and keeping a boyfriend. She had been working on her dissertation full time for 3 years but had not yet decided on a topic. She was an attractive, well-dressed, and very talented woman with many friends and an active life.

The patient was cooperative in therapy in the sense of coming on time, talking, and paying for sessions. However, there was almost constant negativity and sarcasm in her interactions with the therapist. She stated repeatedly that the therapist was not sufficiently warm or outgoing, so that the patient never felt helped or even cared for. When 3 years went by with no progress toward finishing the PhD or finding a husband, both patient and therapist were feeling impatient and hopeless.

Ms. M. came from a home where the parents were quite intrusive and negative toward their children, often overstimulating them with stories of their own unhappiness as adults. The parents were nasty and critical with each other, although they had an active social life and many close friends. The father was a successful lawyer and the mother a frustrated social worker who had not pursued a career after her children were born. When Ms. M. was 18 years old, her mother developed breast cancer and died 3 years later. The maternal grandmother had also died of breast cancer. Ms. M. had one sibling, an older sister, who remained single into her late 30s but was a successful lawyer with the same specialization as her father. During the course of the therapy, the patient's father developed heart problems and when she was 29 years old, 2 years into the treatment, he died suddenly, leaving a large estate to his two children. Ms. M. had been very close to her father and he had been enthusiastic about her PhD aspirations, so his death was quite a blow to her. She spoke about him in only positive terms and became depressed, feeling there was no reason to go on living if she had no parents to appreciate her accomplishments.

The therapist had learned early on that a positive or even neutral attitude did not help this patient. Ms. M. experienced such an approach as unreal and meaningless. Apparently it did not sufficiently replicate the atmosphere of her parental home, thus failing to cathect and activate her earlier memories (Kubie, 1963).

Ms. M. suspected that the therapist wanted her to finish her PhD and she was correct in her suspicion. The therapist was sick of hearing her whine and postpone life plans until the completion of her degree. Given the negative relationship with the patient, the therapist decided to act paradoxically and she stated, with some force: "I have decided that it would be a grave error for you to finish that degree. Your unconscious mind equates this struggle with life because all the time that your parents were alive you were struggling. Now that your father is gone, there is no one left to appreciate your work. If you stop working now, you can keep your parents alive emotionally; if you finish, you may feel even worse than you do already." This intervention, where the therapist acted in a negative and intrusive manner, was an imitation of the early objects. The therapist never believed the interpretation and it was unpleasant for her to talk in such a manner, but it seemed worth a try.

The patient was fascinated by the intervention and over the next year, she kept asking the therapist if it were really true. The therapist took a stance of refusing to discuss the idea in detail, stating that it was just a feeling she had. This stance gave the patient space to develop her own fantasies at the same time as the absence of further information stopped her from developing negativity. The intervention was always repeated with confidence by the therapist when she was questioned.

Within a year, the patient finished her degree. This accomplishment helped her to get a satisfying job and her life improved a great deal. There was less whining and complaining in the therapy.

This is an example of a patient who developed a negative personality as a means to protect herself from painful stimulation early in life. Her negative style kept her repeating the early experiences as a young adult. The therapist acted in a negative manner in order to become an emotionally legitimate object, and gave a paradoxical intervention to facilitate change.

Case No. 3–An Indifferent Patient

Ms. Q., a 27-year-old single woman, came to treatment with a female therapist seeking advice about how to help her mother deal with her depression following the death of the mother's father. After the initial session, this subject has never been the focus in 4 years of therapy. The "real" problem was that Ms. Q. had no significant goals in life herself and was quite lost about what to do. She had graduated magna cum laude from an Ivy League college without working particularly hard and then had gone on to graduate school in three totally different areas, dropping out of each program within the first 2 years. She was currently unemployed and living off a monthly stipend from her parents. She had many friends but no boyfriend, and she expressed no wish to find a boyfriend.

The family background was upper middle class. The father was a dentist and had several other dentists working for him, so that his income was substantial. The mother had been an English major and a political activist in her youth but had not pursued outside activity after her children were born. The father worked long hours but hated his work; the mother constantly expressed regret about what she could have done in life.

Despite several years of therapy, the parents were unhappily married and survived with each other by maintaining a formal distance. The patient had one older brother who was the focus of her parents' concern. He had also attended graduate school unsuccessfully and had been unemployed for 3 years. In contrast to Ms. Q., the brother had never done well in school, and the parents had always worried about him. He had had drug problems (cocaine and marijuana) at various periods and had never accomplished anything in life. The parents provided him financial support but he spent more money than they wanted to provide. They resented supporting him although they did not mind helping their daughter financially.

The patient talked easily in therapy and seemed to enjoy it. She never expressed any interest in the therapist but was content to talk about the events of her own life every week. Nothing much happened in her outside life for 2 years. The therapist enjoyed the sessions but was not particularly involved and sometimes thought about suggesting that the number of sessions be reduced. When the therapist became aware that the familial pattern of indifference to the patient was being repeated, she decided to try to make a change to bring some energy into the treatment. The major resistance seemed to be a resistance to transference, so the interventions took the form of drawing attention to the relationship to the therapist. When the patient talked about returning to her last graduate program, the therapist asked "What do you think I would do?" When the patient did return to this graduate program, the therapist stated, "You know, I have a bias toward your finishing this program." When the patient talked about her friends' envy of the financial subsidy her parents gave her, the therapist said, "Well it isn't really that much money. I know a lot of people who get more than that from their parents." The last intervention was meant to help the patient to stop making herself "different" from everyone else, and left room for fantasies that the therapist was just as well off as she was. The therapist also told her that her parents had not given her examples of how to work and to be happy in life but that she could learn that in therapy. The therapist encouraged Ms. Q. to attend all her sessions and schedule various trips out of town so that they would not conflict, giving the feeling that every session was very important.

As the therapist forced more involvement in the relationship, the patient began to do better in outside life. She returned to graduate school and finally finished a degree. She obtained work in her field and got closer to financial independence from her parents. In one session she stated, "I had felt all my life that I could do anything and now I know my limitations. This is better." Ms. Q. continued in treatment and continued to do better in life but she did not form a significant sexual relationship until 2 more years had passed.

This case is an example of the patient who has been neglected in life because she had so many strengths that she never caused trouble. The parents never pressured her to make choices and, in fact, they supported her continued ambivalence in life by giving her unlimited financial support. She needed to have the feeling that somebody was worried about her and wanted her to make some choices. The fact that she was female contributed to her problem because the parents felt that she could achieve an identity when she married, failing to assess the changing social situation where today's talented women are not settling for marriage alone. The repetition of getting by without major accomplishment was reversed when the therapist helped the patient to become interested in their relationship. The patient modeled herself on the therapist and made some choices in her career which enabled her to have career success. As in the other case studies, the change in external object relations came after the change in career pattern.

REFERENCES

Barth, J. (1967). *The end of the road.* New York: Doubleday.

Erikson, E. (1968). *Identity: Youth and crisis.* New York: Norton.

Hendrick, I. (1943). Work and the pleasure principle. *Psychoanalytic Quarterly, 12*, 39-48.

Kohut, H. (1977). *The restoration of the self.* Madison, CT: International Universities Press.

Kohut, H. (1979). The two analyses of Mr. Z. *International Journal of Psychoanalysis 60*, 3-27.

Kubie, L. (1963). The central affective potential and its trigger mechanism. *Counterpoint: Libidinal object and subject* (pp. 49-87). New York: International Universities Press.

Meerloo, J., & Nelson, M.C. (1965). *Transference and trial adaptation.* Springfield, IL: Charles C Thomas.

Nelson, M.C. (1968). On the therapeutic redirection of energy and affects. In M.C. Nelson (Ed.), *Roles and paradigms in psychotherapy* (pp. 19-44). New York: Grune and Stratton.

Padel, J. (1987). Object relational approach. In. J. Fosshage and C. Loew (Eds.), *Dream interpretation: A comparative study.* Rev. edition. (pp. 125-248). New York: P.M.A. Publishing Corporation.

The Personal Valuation of Promiscuity: A Method of Investigation

Hubert J.M. Hermans
Els Hermans-Jansen

SUMMARY. In this article a method of self-investigation, devised for the study of personal meaning in the context of one's own history, is applied to promiscuous behavior. The method invites clients to investigate their own life in terms of valuations, a *valuation* being any unit of meaning that has a positive, negative, or ambivalent meaning in the eyes of the client. The valuation may concern any events occurring in his or her past, present, and future (e.g., a dear memory, an insoluble problem, an attractive person, an unreachable goal). The personal meaning of promiscuous behavior can be understood as part of the client's organized valuation system. In the case studied here, promiscuity was found to be an effort to fill the void created by the early loss of a father.

We have two reservations about the general use of the term *promiscuity.* First, there is a strong dependence on the values of a par-

---

Dr. Hubert J.M. Hermans is Professor of Personality Psychology at the University of Nijmegen. In the '60s he worked as a test constructor in the field of achievement motivation and fear of failure. Partly as a reaction to his dissatisfaction with work in this field, his interests shifted in the '70s to the basic problem of human valuation. He has devised a self-confrontation method together with the underlying valuation theory as a procedure for self-investigation and organization.

Mailing address: University of Nijmegen, P.O. Box 9104, 6500 HE Nijmegen, The Netherlands.

Ms. Els Hermans-Jansen was originally a youth worker before she started to study pedagogy. Later she qualified herself as a psychotherapist and has a private practice in Berg en Dall in which she applies the self-confrontation method as a procedure for assessment and intervention and as an instrument for the evaluation of the change process.

The authors thank Willem van Gilst for his statistical advice, and Lee Ann Weeks for her detailed editorial comments.

ticular society or epoch. Second, as a label promiscuity in fact covers a heterogeneous set of sexual and social behaviors.

The value-laden character of the promiscuity concept can best be demonstrated by pointing to the 1950s, when the dominant cultural sexual norm implied that premarital or extramarital sex was wrong, particularly for women. As Spreadbury (1982) observes, such behaviors often resulted in the label of "promiscuous" by one's family, friends, and especially one's enemies. One knew that having premarital or extramarital sex–regardless of the nature of the relationship–would lead to a negative label. In our time, however, having sex with many different partners is evaluated from the perspective of physical danger: The life-threatening, epidemiological consequences of AIDS have made themselves clear. Promiscuity is not so much seen as counter to the idea of marriage but as a threat to life.

The term "promiscuity" is commonly associated with "engaging in sexual relations with a considerable above-average number of partners" (Goode & Troiden, 1980). In this sense, however, the term covers a heterogeneous set of behaviors and this heterogeneity may even weaken the utility of the term. For example, Fluker (1983) wonders if the average prostitute who certainly regards herself as a professional, should be considered promiscuous. And perhaps Don Juan would have been most outraged if he was accused of anything so vulgar. In Mozart's version he had 2065 conquests on his list in which he took great pride. In homosexual circles having contact with many partners is quite common. Some male homosexuals have a scorecard of a thousand and the majority have at least 100 partners. And in some peril of life there are developmental reasons for frequently changing social and sexual contacts. Teenagers may change boyfriends and girlfriends quite frequently, although they usually have only one at a time and therefore consider themselves to always be faithful (Fluker, 1983).

In the light of the above considerations we want to emphasize that it is very difficult, if not impossible, to psychologically characterize the general phenomenon of promiscuity. It seems to be more fruitful to ask what is the meaning of promiscuous behavior for a particular person in a particular situation? In other words, when we observe that an individual is engaging in sexual relations with a considerable number of sexual partners, this is not more than a factual observation. To understand the significance of this behavior for the individual, psychological investigation in the context of his or her own personal history is needed.

The purpose of this article is to present an assessment method for the investigation of the personal meaning of promiscuous behavior. The method is one of self-investigation, where the client is invited as a responsible individual to cooperate with a psychotherapist in the assessment of a particular problem in the context of his or her total life situation. This is done in such a way that the client is not only actively engaged in the assessment process but also in the change process. In the present study, we report on the self-confrontation of a middle-aged man involved in many sexual relationships.

The client is a 47-year-old man, who, although married and father of two children, had continual extramarital contacts with other women. The frequency of these contacts was so high and so disrupting to the contact with his wife and children that friends tried to persuade the woman to leave her husband. Before making her decision, the wife proposed therapy. The therapy was for the husband and wife to each, independently, perform a self-investigation and then discuss the results in cooperation with the psychotherapist who assisted them in performing the self-investigations. As the results indicate, there was clearly an experience of unfulfilled love due to the early loss of the father underlying the strongly self-enhancing behavior of the man in this case. His changing contacts with many women was obviously an attempt to fill a void. As will be seen, this diagnosis was formulated by the man, *himself,* in close cooperation with the psychotherapist. This insight had significant impact on his contact with his wife and led to the decision of husband and wife to stay together.

In the following a description of valuation theory–the theory underlying the self-investigation method–will be presented; the self-investigation method itself will be described; and the application of the method to an actual case of promiscuity will be discussed.

VALUATION THEORY: ORGANIZING ONE'S SELF

Valuation theory (Hermans, 1987a; 1988; 1989) was, as a self theory, developed for the study of individual experiences, their ordering into a meaning system, and their development over time. The theory's view of the person is inspired by earlier philosophical-phenomenological thinking (James, 1890; Merleau-Ponty, 1945) and personality is conceived of as an *organized process*, as an articulated set of personally ordered historical events. The "process" aspect refers to the historical nature of human experience and implies a spatio-temporal orientation: A person lives in the present, and is therefore oriented from a specific point in time and space to the past and to the future. The "organizational" aspect is supposed to emphasize that the person, through orienting to different aspects of his or her spatio-temporal situation and self-reflection, creates a composite whole in which experiences are differentially weighted.

The theory's central concept, *valuation*, includes anything people find to be of importance when thinking about their life situation. A valuation is any unit of meaning that has a positive (pleasant), negative (unpleasant), or ambivalent (both pleasant and unpleasant) value in the eyes of the individual. It can include a broad range of phenomena: a dear memory, a difficult problem, an admired person, a disturbing dream, an unreachable goal, the anticipated death of a significant other, and so forth. Through the process of self-reflection, valuations are organized into a single system. And depending on the individual's orientation to the past, the present, and the future, different valuations emerge.

An essential feature of valuation theory is the assumption that each valuation has an affective connotation. More specifically, each valuation implies an affective modality: a specific pattern of affect. When we know which types of affect are implied by a particular valuation, we know something about the valuation itself. Note that affect in this theory is not considered a direct "result" of cognitive processing but inherent in cognition. Affect is considered the movement implicit in a valuation and clearly tied to the spatial character of a valuation (e.g., joy as "going up," despondency as "going down," strength as "getting a grip on things," and intimacy as "getting into something or somebody").

In order to capture certain differences in the functioning of the affective component of the valuation system, the latent-manifest distinction was introduced into valuation theory (Hermans, Hermans-Jansen, & Van Gilst, 1985). It is assumed that a small set of basic motives is represented latently in the affective component of a valuation. These basic motives are assumed to be similar across individuals and to be continuously active within each individual moving through time and space. At the manifest level, valuations vary phenomenologically not only between individuals but also within a single individual across time and space.

The model presented thus far allows for the inclusion of different theoretically well-founded motives. In the research concerning valuation theory two basic motives have thus far been developed to characterize the affective component of the valuation system: the striving for self-enhancement, or S-motive (i.e., self-maintenance and self-expansion), and the longing for contact and union with the other, or O-motive (i.e., contact with other people and the surrounding world). This distinction resulted from a review of a number of researchers' conceptions of the basic duality of human experience: Bakan (1966), who viewed agency and communion as fundamental dynamic principles; Angyal (1965), with his concepts of autonomy (self-determination) and homonomy (self-surrender); and Klages (1948) who considered Bindung (solidification) and Lösung (dissolution) as basic motives of human character. More recently, McAdams (1985) has identified the distinction between power and intimacy within a narrative context, again suggesting the basicness of the S- and O-motives. This does not, however, mean that other theoretically well-founded motives cannot be incorporated into valuation theory.

To illustrate the use of this model, when a person values something he or she always feels something about it and in these feelings the basic motives are reflected. When a valuation (e.g., "I enjoy watching my daughter play with her toys") represents a gratification of the O-motive, then the person experiences a feeling of tenderness or intimacy in connection with the valuation. In a similar way a valuation (e.g., "I passed a difficult test") can function as a gratification of the S-motive. Feelings of strength and pride experienced in connection with the valuation are indicators of this motive. The affective component of the valuation system can be seen as the representation on the manifest level of the motivational base on the latent level.

The latent-manifest distinction is particularly useful when it comes to analyzing the narrative structure of the self. When, for example, somebody tells about his past sports achievements and later on shifts the subject to his plan to write a book, this shift represents only a difference on the manifest level. From the perspective of the latent level the same self-enhancement motive may be guiding his two interests. Similarly, somebody can be engaged in different activities (e.g., singing in a group, caring for a friend, enjoying nature) whereas all these orientations stem from the same contact motive. And, of course, a person may shift from the one motive to the other motive in the course of life.

On the basis of the foregoing considerations, we chose the following starting points for the study of promiscuous behavior.

1. Promiscuous behavior has personal meaning; this behavior is attributed a positive, negative, or ambivalent value by the individual as part of his or her self-reflection.
2. The valuation of promiscuous behavior is contextual; that is, together with the other valuations from the same individual, promiscuous behavior is part of an organized valuation system.
3. The valuation of promiscuous behavior is rooted in a latent motivational base. Promiscuous behavior is one of the rich phenomenological variety of valuations that receive their organization and direction from a limited number of basic psychological motives.

STRUCTURE OF THE SELF-CONFRONTATION METHOD

The self-confrontation method, as a procedure for self-investigation, is based on valuation theory. It was designed to study the relation between valuations and types of affect and the way both variables are organized into a structured whole (Hermans, 1987a). The structured whole is reflected by a matrix where the rows represent the valuations and the columns the affects (see Appendix for an example).

The procedure involves three parts: (a) elicitation of a set of valuations; (b) associating each valuation with a standardized set of affect-denoting terms, and (c) discussion of the results with the client.

Elicitation of Valuations

The valuations (i.e., rows in the matrix) are elicited by a series of open-ended questions. The questions ask for important units of meaning from the past, present, and future. They invite people to reflect on their life situation in such a way that they feel free to mention those concerns that are most relevant from the perspective of the present situation. The main questions are presented in Table 1; additional questions may be used depending on the aims of the investigation and the topic. The subjects are greatly free in their interpretation of the questions. The intention is that they stimulate the subjects to tell something that they consider as important in their own self-narrative. The subjects are encouraged to phrase the valuations *in their own terms* so that the formulations are as much as possible in agreement with the intended meaning. The typical grammatical expression is the sentence. When the person is not able or does not want to formulate the valuation as a sentence, he or she is permitted to express it with just a few words or with a single word. A quick response is not required and there is no one-to-one relation between question and answer. The person is encouraged to mention all valuations that come to mind and, typically, each question leads to more than one valuation. The aim of this part of the self-investigation is to arrive at an exhaustive survey of relevant experiences.

At the end of the interview subjects are asked if the survey contains all the experiences that they consider important from their present perspective. If something is missing, they can add this. At the end of this procedure people may have differing numbers of valuations, but in most cases they are between 20 and 40.

Promiscuous behavior can, like any other behavior, be included in the self-investigation when the person finds it of interest. In this case the significance of the behavior is phrased as a sentence, which can later be studied in the context of the other valuations.

Table 1

Questions of the Self-Confrontation Method

set 1: The Past

These questions are intended to guide you to some aspect of your past life that is of great importance to you.

-- Was there something in your past that has been of major importance or significance for your life and which still plays an important part today?

-- Was there, in the past, (a) person(s), an experience, or circumstance that greatly influenced your life and still appreciably affects your present existence?

You are free to go back into the past as far as you like.

set 2: The Present

This set is also composed of two questions that will lead you, after a certain amount of thinking, to formulate a response:

-- Is there in your present life something that is of major importance for, or exerts a great influence on, your existence?

-- Is there in your present life (a) person(s) or a circumstance which exerts a significant influence on you?

set 3: The Future

The following questions will again be found to guide you to a response:

-- Do you foresee something that will be of great importance for, or of major influence on, your future life?

-- Do you feel that (a) certain person(s) or circumstance will exert a great influence on your future life?

-- Is there a future goal or object which you expect to play an important role in your life?

You are free to look as far ahead as you wish.

Connection with Affect Terms

In the second part of the investigation, a standard list of affect terms (columns in the matrix, see Appendix) is presented to the subject. Concentrating on the first valuation, the subject indicates on a 0-5 scale to what extent he or she experiences each affect in relation to this specific valuation (0 = *not at all*, 1 = *a little bit*, 2 = *to some extent*, 3 = *rather much*, 4 = *much*, and 5 = *very much*). The subject, working alone now (with paper-and-pencil or on-line), rates each valuation with the same list of affect terms; the different valuations can then be compared according to their affective profiles. The list used in the present study is a most recent one (i.e., a condensed form of the list used by Hermans, 1987b), and contains 16 affect terms (see Table 2). This list was selected on the grounds that it contains the minimum number of affect terms that nevertheless in combination permit the maximum of information about the motivational aspects of the valuation system to be gained. Of course other and more elaborate lists can be used depending on the affective phenomena the psychotherapist wants to investigate, the client population, and the setting. On the basis of the matrix a variety of indices can be calculated. The indices relevant to the present study are summarized in the following paragraphs.

1. Index S is the sum of the scores for the affect terms expressing self-enhancement: Numbers 2, 5, 11, and 14 of Table 2.
2. Index O is the sum of the scores for the affect terms expressing contact and union with the other: Numbers 7, 8, 10, and 12. For each valuation, the S-O difference is then determined. When the experience of self-enhancement is stronger than the experience of contact with the other, S > O. When contact with the other prevails, O > S. When both kinds of experience coexist, S = O.
3. Index P is the sum of the general-positive (pleasant) affect scores: Numbers 1, 3, 6, and 16.
4. Index N is the sum of the general-negative (unpleasant) affect scores: Numbers: 4, 9, 13, and 15. For each valuation, the P-N difference is then calculated. This difference indicates the well-being that the person experiences in relation to the specific valuation. Well-being is positive when P > N, negative when N > P, and ambivalent when P = N. (Note that the scores for each of the four indices S, O, P, and N range from 0 to 20).
5. For the assessment of the extent of generalization (G) of a valuation within the system, the following question is asked

at the end of the valuation construction phase: "How do I *generally* feel these days?" This question does not ask for a specific valuation but is devised to assess the "general feeling." The person answers directly with the list of affect terms that was used for the characterization of the valuations. This pattern of scores is filled in the matrix as the final row (see Appendix). The product-moment correlation between the pattern of affects that belong to a specific valuation (any row in the matrix) and the pattern of affects that belong to the general feeling (final row in the matrix) is a measure of the extent of generalization of this valuation. The more positive the correlation is, the more this valuation is supposed to generalize within the system. (For validity and reliability data of the type of indices described see Hermans, 1987b, p. 166 and pp. 169-171).

Discussion of Results with the Client

The discussion of the results usually follows one week after the first two parts of the self-investigation. After the construction of the valuations (about one-and-a-half hours in the case of 25 valuations) and the filling in of the affect matrix (also about one-and-a-half hours for the same number of valuations), most people are tired and need time to digest the many impressions, associations, and thoughts that have occurred. In this week, the interviewer (who may

Table 2

Affect Terms Used in the Self-Confrontation Method

1. Joy	9. Unhappiness
2. Self-Esteem	10. Tenderness
3. Happiness	11. Self-Confidence
4. Worry	12. Intimacy
5. Strength	13. Despondency
6. Enjoyment	14. Pride
7. Caring	15. Disappointment
8. Love	16. Inner Calm

also be the psychotherapist) performs a qualitative analysis (studying the content of the valuations, with proper attention to their relation) and a quantitative analysis (computation and interpretation of indices).

The discussion has the quality of an intensive self-reflection on the part of the client and a profound dialogue with the interviewer. Client and interviewer base their discussion on the overall picture provided by the system in which valuations that refer to past, present, and future are contracted so that new relations, hitherto hidden, can become visible. Such an overall picture is a specific property of the self-confrontation method; that is, short discussions dispersed over time often have a narrower scope. Moreover, in the discussion, the valuations are enriched by the information derived from the separate affects, the affective indices, combination of indices, and comparison of affect patterns of different valuations. The basic motives are also explained. All this information is used to evaluate one's own behavior, to generate new ideas, to take new initiatives, and to develop a sense of direction in daily life. The discussion is necessarily confined to one session. By preference, it is continued in successive sessions where dally experiences can be compared with content and organization of the valuation system. In this way a beginning can be made of a reorganization of the system.

In essence, the self-confrontation method represents a dialogical model between professional and client. Both are seen as experts, each with their specific expertise. Clients are considered as expert in the knowledge that concerns their own experiences. Clients have the largest databank available of their own life and are uniquely able to communicate about those things that they consider relevant in their particular situation. The professional is primarily an expert with respect to general concepts, theories, and corresponding methodology and has experience with other clients; therefore, he or she has insight into phenomena and processes at a more general level.

The self-confrontation method creates a platform on which these two experts meet each other. The client presents his or her valuation system; the professional offers a series of affect terms, selected to represent certain basic motives. These affects, their combination, and the following discussion permit a new perspective on the valuation system to be taken and can, in principle, highlight the more subtle of implicit aspects of the system. The resulting information and insight can be used by the clients to (re-)evaluate their behavior, including their sexual and social behavior, as we shall see in the following section.

A CASE STUDY: FILLING THE VACUUM

As already mentioned in the introduction to this article, our client together with his wife contacted a psychotherapist (the second author) in a period of serious marital problems. The man worked for the army and the woman was a housewife. Both had completed high school. They had no psychiatric history.

The man's many love affairs played a major role in their decision to ask for psychotherapeutic assistance. The extramarital contacts had not stopped even though the wife had moved out of the house and was considering divorce. They discussed their problem with some of their friends who advised the woman to get a divorce. When she did not do this and the man continued with his affairs, the friends severed contact with the couple. It was this event that gave rise to the contact with the psychotherapist.

The husband and wife both performed a self-investigation according to the described procedure and discussed the results with the psychotherapist, independently and later together. The man, on whom we will focus, formulated a total of 29 valuations. In order to characterize his valuation system, we present three representative valuation subgroups in Table 3.

1. Consider valuations nos. 1-3, where the experience of self-enhancement is stronger than the experience of contact and union with the other (S > O) and the character of the valuations is neither very positive (P) nor very negative (N). The content of these valuations typically refers to the past and emphasizes that the man was *forced* to be autonomous both at home (no. 1) and at school (no. 2), and that he also must perform autonomously in his work situation (no. 3).
2. Consider valuations nos. 4-6, where contact and union is more strongly emphasized than self-enhancement (O > S). At the

same time, the negative affect (N) is stronger than the positive affect (P). This peculiar combination of index scores (low S, high O; low P, high N) is known to be indicative of a *fugit amor* experience (Hermans, Hermans-Jansen, & Van Gilst, 1987). In such a situation, the individual has a loving orientation toward somebody (or something) who is nevertheless unreachable. *(Fugit amor* is the title of a statue from the French sculptor Rodin which was inspired by the unhappy love story of Paolo and Francesca in Dante's *La Divina Commedia.)* In valuation no. 4, the client mentions a feeling of mental isolation and inner disintegration. In valuation no. 5, he refers to his inability to limit his sexual aspirations. (Note that the client does not mention in his self-investigation his love affairs in a more specific way, but rather considers them implied in a *broader* meaning structure that centers around the problem of mental isolation and his inability to break out of it.)

3. Finally, consider valuations nos. 7-9, where the experience of self-enhancement and contact/union are both high and experienced in a very positive way (P > N). In these valuations our client refers to the gratifying contact with his family members and some friends (high O), contact that also contributes to his self-respect (high S).

When these three subgroups are compared, the second group (nos. 4-6) is found to show a very strong degree of generalization (see index G). This means that despite the gratifying contact with his wife and some friends (nos. 7-9), the problem of mental isolation and unfulfilled desire still dominates in this man's valuation system.

All of the above findings–the content of the valuations and their affective organization–were discussed with the client in detail. In this discussion he was also asked about the exact nature of his self-enhancement and how this might be related to his feelings of isolation. In particular, the question that his seemingly self-confident behavior in his military work-setting and social contacts was simply a means to hide or suppress his feelings of social isolation and unfulfilled desire for emotional contact was raised. When the dis-

Table 3

Representative Valuations, General Feeling, and Scores on the Affective Indices

	Valuation	S	O	P	N	G
1.	With father's death and mother's work I missed out on parental guidance and had to find my own way	12	5	4	9	.01
2.	With the decision of the principal, I was suddenly shoved out of the patriarchal boarding-school into the "full of life" (choosing yourself whether you want to do something or not)	12	6	8	7	-.33
3.	My military background has influenced my way of problem solving: making decisions and judgements with little or no discussion	14	7	8	6	-.41
4.	The way my life is now has a chaotic effect on me: I live in mental dissatisfaction, a sort of isolation - I'm falling apart	4	14	0	17	.96
5.	I think alot about myself and norms: why I can't set any limitations for myself, yell "stop" to myself in time	7	15	3	15	.73
6.	I'm worried about Mark [son]; he is isolating himself	8	18	4	17	.84
7.	I have good contact with Cynthia [daughter]	16	18	15	4	-.47
8.	I feel myself to be one with Sandra [wife]	18	20	20	1	-.66
9.	I have a trusting relationship with Steve and Carla [friends] and feel close to them	12	10	13	3	-.62
	General feeling	4	12	3	16	----

S = affect referring to self-enhancement; O =-affect referring to contact with the other; P = positive affect; N = negative affect; G = generalization cussion centered on valuation no. 1, which the client isolated as the origin of his problems, it was decided to investigate this valuation in more detail.

In order to examine its motivational structure, valuation no. 1 was subdivided into four parts, which were separately rated with the same affect terms used for the other valuations. The results, presented in Table 4, show that the first part of this valuation ("my father's death") has the same *fugit amor* pattern of affect reported for the second group of valuations in Table 3. As can be seen in Table 4, it is also this part of the valuation that has the greatest degree of generalization. The other parts of valuation no. 1 have a strongly self-enhancing quality, however, which does not get generalized. This configuration suggests that the self-enhancing quality is intended to compensate for the experience of unfulfilled desire: valuation no. 1 is organized in such a way that a specific experience (father's death) is forcefully transformed into specific self-enhancing activities. In reality, however, this may only be an attempt to overcome a painful experience that has simply never been worked through.

At the end of the discussion with the psychotherapist the client was invited to phrase in his own words what he had learned from his self-investigation. He formulated the following statement: "Because of my achievement behavior and constant running I lack a base for my development, that is, a way of reaching out to the other, communication; I have defended myself to a great extent in order to avoid being vulnerable." This conclusion and its implications were discussed in another session with his wife, who in turn discussed the results of her investigation with her husband. Finally, they decided to continue their relationship and to try again.

SOME FEATURES OF THE SELF-CONFRONTATION METHOD

In the present study we proposed a theory-based, idiographic method for examining the meaning of specific behaviors in the context of the client's personal history. In the case considered here, the client came to realize that his promiscuous behavior was rather a futile attempt to fill a void created by the early loss of a parent.

Table 4

Valuation 1 Subdivided into Four Subparts, General Feeling, and Scores on the Affective Indices

Valuation Subparts	S	O	P	N	G
1. My father's death	3	14	0	17	.92
2. My mother's work	11	8	2	11	.44
3. I have missed parental guidance	11	4	2	11	.27
4. I had to seek out my own way	14	10	8	9	-.22
General feeling	4	12	3	16	----

S = affect referring to self-enhancement; O = affect referring to contact with the other; P = positive affect; N = negative affect; G = generalization

This case study greatly resembles Eber's (1981) general, theoretical analysis of *Don Juanism,* which he describes as a disorder of the self. On the basis of Kohut's (1977) psychoanalytic psychology of the self, Eber argues that promiscuous behavior can be understood as an effort to fill in the structural void left by faulty interactions between self and parental figures (Eber, 1981, p. 309). Also the disintegration anxiety, which Kohut (1977) describes as the dread experienced when the autonomy of the self is threatened, could clearly be assessed as a property of our client's self (see valuation no. 4 in Table 3).

A difference between our approach and that of Eber, however, is that we have not formulated any specific *a priori* assumption about the concept of promiscuity or Don Juanism but, rather, invited the client to examine his own life himself. In the case study described here neither the interviewer nor the client had any theoretically specific preconceptions about the concept of promiscuity. Within the open framework of valuation theory and the corresponding methodology, we *empirically discovered* the existence of a void and disintegration anxiety. Note that this realization was brought about by the specific expertise of the client as a knower of himself in combination with the professional insights and methodology of the psychotherapist.

There are three distinctive features of the self-confrontation method that should be mentioned at this point in order to better understand the approach: its emphasis on individuality, contextuality, and the gradual transition between assessment and change.

An adequate explication of the term *individuality* requires, as Harré and Lamb (1983) have explained, distinguishing between two different contrasts associated with the word. The first contrast is that between "whole" and "part," where individuality refers to a whole composed of parts that cannot be isolated or abstracted from the whole. The origin of this meaning is to be found in the Latin word "individuum" or the Greek "atomos," referring to that which is undivided or indivisible. In spite of its etymological origin, "individual" in the sense of an indivisible, unitary entity does not preclude either a multiplicity of attributes or a complexity of structure (cf. Harré & Lamb, 1983). The second contrast opposes "specific" and "general" as hierarchical terms used to order species and kinds. In such a series the individual occupies the lowest level because it cannot be further divided logically. Individuality in this sense means "specific" and refers to the individual as a particular person. In the approach proposed in the present article the phenomenon of promiscuity was translated as part of an organized process of valuation, and–as we have demonstrated in our case study–promiscuity was attributed an individual quality in the two senses just described: (a) the meaning of promiscuous behavior cannot be isolated from the organized whole of the valuation system, which functions as the reference system for its understanding; and (b) promiscuous behavior can only be properly understood when it is seen as a manifestation of general motives in a particular individual moving through time and space.

Closely related to the concept of individuality is the issue of *contextuality*. As we have seen in our case study, the individual creates a text about himself, that can have reference to past, present, and future events or experiences, a self-narrative (Crites, 1986; Sarbin, 1986). Each part of such a text is contextualized, just as a sentence receives a fuller meaning in the context of a discourse. In our case, the client has constructed a series of valuations and these valuations together provide the context for a more complete understanding of the meaning of his promiscuous behavior. It is a distinctive feature of the self-confrontation method, as we have said, that experiences normally dispersed in time are concentrated at one moment. And as Rychlak (1988) has argued, the essential ingredient in meaning is the perception of relations. The condensation of valuations into a single system during the course of a self-investigation indeed allows hitherto implicit or hidden relations to become visible.

Finally, the self-confrontation method strongly appeals to the client's own responsibility and the self-organizing capacity of the individual, which allow for *a gradual transition between assessment and change*. For example, questions of the type presented in Table 1 are not posed as something "the doctor wants to know about you," but as questions that one must ask oneself as part of the process of self-reflection. The questions are open in the sense that the client is encouraged to actively construe the answers to satisfactorily fit his or her own perspective, and at the end of the self-investigation clients are even invited to summarize the results in their own words. This step may be crucial for creating a bridge between the assessment situation and the daily life situation or–when necessary–further therapy. Such summary statements regarding the essence of the promiscuous behavior, or any other behavior found to be problematic, motivate clients to look for possible changes.

REFERENCES

Angyal, A. (1965). *Neurosis and treatment: A holistic theory*. New York: Wiley.

Bakan, D. (1966). *The duality of human existence*. Chicago: Rand-McNally.

Crites, S. (1986). Storytime: Recollecting the past and projecting the future. In R. Sarbin (Ed.), *Narrative psychology: The storied nature of human conduct*, (pp. 152-173). New York: Praeger.

Eber, M. (1981). Don Juanism; A disorder of the self. *Bulletin of the Menninger Clinic, 45*, 307-316.

Fluker, J.L. (1983). The perils of promiscuity. *Journal of Psychosomatic Research, 27*, 153-156.

Goode, E., & Troiden, R.R. (1980). Correlates and accompaniments of promiscuous sex among male homosexuals. *Psychiatry, 43*, 51-59.

Harré, R., & Lamb, R. (1983). *The encyclopedic dictionary of psychology*. Oxford: Basil Blackwell.

Hermans, H.J.M. (1987a). Self as organized system of valuations: Toward a dialogue with the person. *Journal of Counseling Psychology, 34*, 10-19.

Hermans, H.J.M. (1987b). The dream in the process of valuation: A method of interpretation. *Journal of Personality and Social Psychology, 53*, 163-175.

Hermans, H.J.M. (1988). On the integration of idiographic and nomothetic research method in the study of personal meaning. *Journal of Personality, 56*, 785-812.

Hermans, H.J.M. (1989). The meaning of life as an organized process. *Psychotherapy, 26*(1), 11-22.

Hermans, H.J.M., Hermans-Jansen, E., & Van Gilst, W. (1985). *De grondmotieven van het menselijk bestaan* [The basic motives of human existence]. Lisse: Swets & Zeitlinger.

Hermans, H.J.M., Hermans-Jansen, E., & Van Gilst, W. (1987). The *fugit amor* experience in the process of valuation: A self-confrontation with an unreachable other. *British Journal of Psychology, 78*, 465-481.

James, W. (1890). *The principles of psychology*, (Vol. 1). London: Macmillan.

Klages, L. (1948). *Charakterkunde* (Characterology). Zürich, Switzerland: Hirzel.

Kohut, H. (1977). *The restoration of the self*. New York: International Universities Press.

McAdams, D.P. (1985). *Power, intimacy, and the life story: Personological inquiries into identity*. Chicago: Dorsey Press. (Reprinted by Guilford Press).

Merleau-Ponty, M. (1945). *Phénoménologie de la perception [Phenomenology of perception*]. Paris: Gallimard.

Rychlak, J.F. (1988). *The psychology of rigorous humanism* (2nd ed.). New York: New York University Press.

Sarbin, T.R. (1986). The narrative as a root metaphor for psychology. In T.R. Sarbin (Ed.), *Narrative psychology: The storied nature of human conduct* (pp. 3-21). New York: Praeger.

Spreadbury, C.L. (1982). The "permissiveness with affection" norm and the labeling of deviants. *Personnel and Guidance Journal, 5*, 280-282.

Appendix

Matrix of Valuation * Affect

Raw Ratings of a Client

Valuation Number	Affect Terms															
	1	2	3	4	5	6	7	8	9	10	11	12	13	14	15	16
1	0	3	2	3	4	1	2	1	2	1	4	1	2	1	2	1
2	1	1	1	3	1	1	2	1	2	1	2	1	3	2	3	3
3	1	4	2	3	3	2	3	3	2	3	4	3	3	3	2	1
4	2	4	2	2	2	3	1	2	1	2	3	1	1	3	3	1
5	1	3	2	3	4	2	3	2	1	1	4	1	1	3	1	3
6	4	4	3	3	3	3	3	2	1	2	4	3	1	3	1	3
7	1	3	1	3	3	1	3	2	2	1	3	1	3	1	3	1
8	1	1	2	3	3	2	3	4	1	3	3	3	1	2	1	2
9	0	1	0	4	1	3	4	5	5	4	1	1	4	1	4	0
10	1	3	3	2	3	1	3	3	1	3	3	3	2	1	1	1
11	1	3	2	4	3	2	3	3	3	3	3	2	3	1	2	1
12	1	2	2	4	2	2	3	2	3	3	1	1	3	1	3	1
13	1	3	1	4	3	1	3	2	3	3	3	2	2	2	3	1
14	5	1	5	4	4	4	4	5	4	5	4	4	3	1	1	2
15	1	1	1	5	3	1	5	5	5	5	3	3	3	1	4	1
16	4	4	4	1	4	3	4	5	1	5	4	4	1	4	1	4
17	2	4	2	3	4	2	3	1	1	1	4	1	1	2	1	4
18	5	4	5	1	4	5	4	5	1	5	4	5	1	1	1	4
19	0	1	1	4	4	1	3	4	4	4	1	4	3	1	4	1
20	1	5	3	4	4	1	4	3	2	2	4	2	1	3	4	1
21	1	4	1	4	3	1	3	2	2	1	3	1	1	3	4	1
22	5	4	5	1	5	5	5	5	0	5	5	5	0	4	0	5
23	4	4	3	1	3	3	0	3	0	3	4	4	1	1	1	3
24	1	4	1	3	3	1	3	2	1	3	1	3	2	1	1	1
25	4	4	4	4	4	1	3	5	4	4	1	4	3	1	0	4
General feeling	1	1	1	4	1	0	3	4	4	4	1	1	4	1	4	1

Note. Rows represent valuations and columns represent affect terms used for the indices S, O, P and N.

AIDS and the Client "In the Fast Lane": Narrative Construction and Reconstruction

Linda Viney
Lynne Bousfield

SUMMARY. This constructivist account of psychotherapy with a sexually promiscuous client comes from a program funded to develop and evaluate psychotherapeutic interventions for people who are HIV-infected or have developed AIDS. Its focus is on narrative construction and reconstruction. The client is shown to tell himself a number of stories which enable him to maintain his often self-defeating behavior which is also potentially dangerous to others. These stories provide him with the guidelines for living his life, and serve many other functions as well. In therapy they are shared with the therapist; and therapist and client together work toward a retelling of these stories, or narrative reconstruction. The account concludes with a comparison of this approach with other apparently similar therapies.

This paper presents a description of psychotherapy with a client who, initially, was promiscuous homosexually, in his eating and

---

Linda Viney, PhD, came to the United States to do her PhD in Clinical Psychology. She directs a university-based training in this area at the University of Wollongong and continues to work with clients in constructivist psychotherapy. This client came from one of her research projects developing therapeutic interventions for people dealing with illness.

Mailing address: Dept. of Psychology, The University of Wollongong, P.O. Box 1144, Wollongong, NSW 2500, Australia.

Lynne Bousfield, BA, is currently a student in that training program. She was awarded the Australian Psychological Society Prize for her BA honors in Psychology. Her approach to therapy is also much influenced by Buddhism. She is the recipient of a Research Scholarship and an Australian Commonwealth Postgraduate Course Award.

drug taking, and in many other ways. However, he took the opportunity to begin to work on this therapeutically when introduced to our program. This program was designed to develop psychotherapy for people who were HIV-infected or had AIDS. It continued for 3 years and was welcomed by the gay community for which it was devised. It employed therapists who were men and women and homosexual and heterosexual. In this case, the therapist was a heterosexual woman. The purpose of this paper is to show how reconstructive therapy was applied with this client to help him understand his interpretations of the world and how they maintained his promiscuous acts, and then to help him reinterpret, so as to be able to change this aspect of his lifestyle. The concept of narrative is added to the traditional concepts of personal construct therapy to produce a reconstructive therapy which focuses on narrative reconstruction.

The paper begins with a brief introduction to reconstructive therapy. This contains an account of the essential concepts of personal construct theory, together with the additional concept of narrative. A definition of narrative is presented, as are a description of its functions and some criteria for judging whether the stories are useful to their teller. It also contains an account of the essential concepts of personal construct therapy, together with narrative reconstruction. A description of narrative reconstruction is provided, as well as some therapeutic techniques for achieving it and some problems that can arise in applying them. Then the client is introduced: his biographical information, his ways of making sense of events such as finding himself to be HIV-infected, his general, guiding narratives and the stories that allowed him to maintain his promiscuity. Some aspects of the slow therapeutic process of his narrative reconstruction are described. In conclusion, this reconstructive therapy is compared with other approaches to the promiscuous client.

RECONSTRUCTIVE THERAPY

The Basic Concepts of Personal Construct Psychology

People use constructs to interpret current events and to anticipate future ones (Kelly, 1955). Constructs are bipolar, so that they provide a choice between different predictions and courses of action. Because people create constructs from their interpretations of past events, they may be unique; however, because many constructs are created through interactions with others, some constructs may be shared. For each person a complex interconnected system of constructs develops, so that some constructs are superordinate, and are more central and influential; and others are subordinate, or more peripheral and lacking influence. When the interpretations from people's construct systems are validated, or confirmed, positive emotion results; when they are invalidated, or disconfirmed, negative emotion results. All constructs can be revised or replaced by other interpretations.

Narrative: An Additional Concept

The concept of narrative is proving useful to personal construct therapists (Mair, 1987; Viney, in press). It refers to the story of events, or the plot of a succession of incidents. This concept provides a focus on people's interpretations that is broader than a single construct but narrower than their entire construct system. It shows constructs in action as people interpret a number of events. We become familiar with the story structure from an early age. The story is a popular medium for teaching moral values as well as for conveying knowledge and information about the world. Literary theory holds three main criteria for the evaluation of narratives. The first criterion is that they integrate separate elements of experience into wholes, and that these wholes have meanings different from their elements (Kurtzman, 1987). The second is that narratives are internally cohesive and consistent (Agar & Hobbs, 1982). The third is that narratives have a time dimension, over which the integration takes place (Schafer, 1983).

There are a variety of definitions of the story in the linguistic, anthropological, and psychological literatures. While these definitions vary in complexity, the arrangement of events across time is the common ingredient. The main aspects of one of the most useful models of narrative structure include the orientation (where the people involved and the setting are introduced); the abstract (which, as its name suggests, is a brief summary of the narrative); the complicating action (the backbone of the story where each sentence seems to be in response to the question, "what happened next?"); the result or resolution (a statement of what finally happened); and the coda (which signals the end of the narrative and brings both the narrator and listener back to the present) (Labov, 1972). Further, interlinked with this narrative structure are evaluations by the storyteller. These evaluations allow the less obvious feelings and emotions of characters to be expressed, as well as emphasize points which the narrator considers to be important. It is clear that some of these features may be more salient to a story's meaning than others; and that individuals will have their own storytelling style that omits or elaborates different aspects of its structure.

Therefore, the criteria for the evaluation of narratives as well as what defines a story requires some modification to be useful psychotherapeutically. For example, people's stories need to provide integration, but not to the point of inflexibility. Also they need to be internally consistent, but only sufficiently so as to provide useful predictions. However, it is the content as well as the structure of narratives which is important. It needs to provide viable choices for people. It also needs to allocate some power to them as well as provide cause for hope. Useful narratives, too, are those that are meaningful, both to the people who tell them and to the people who listen to them.

People act and make their choices in life on the basis of narratives (Sarbin, 1986). Narratives therefore perform many functions in people's lives. They provide purposeful meaning and identity (Macmillan, 1989), as well as continuity and coherence in the face of life's changes (Cohler, 1982). Narratives empower their narrators; and to deprive people of the opportunity to tell their stories only undermines their psychological functioning (Mair, 1990). One reason why extreme life change in the form of crisis can be beneficial to people, is that it provides a way of making a coherent account out of the lack of sense of some people's chaotic lives (Carr, 1985). Self is the center around which people organize their stories, and the construed world is its context. It has proved possible to identify such narratives from interviews (Mishler, 1986; Viney & Bousfield, 1990). Perhaps it is when people's narratives do not fulfill these functions for them that they seek help from psychotherapists.

Since people are continually testing their interpretations by their actions, personal construct therapy can be viewed as a laboratory in which therapists work with clients to experiment with some of their clients' constructs (Kelly, 1955). The aim of such therapy is for clients to become aware of the choices available to them (Fransella, 1985). Such choices come in part from recognition of their own roles as construers and reconstruers (Viney, 1989). The processes by which this occurs have been described in some detail elsewhere (Bannister, 1975; Epting, 1984; Kelly, 1955; Landfield, 1981; Neimeyer & Neimeyer, 1987) and in *The Psychotherapy Patient* (Viney, 1990), as has empirical evidence of its effectiveness (Fransella, 1972; Neimeyer & Neimeyer, 1987; Viney, Benjamin, & Preston, 1988; Viney, Clarke, Bunn, & Benjamin, 1985a, 1985b).

Clients in personal construct therapy can use a number of therapeutic strategies (Viney, Benjamin, & Preston, in press). Loosening interpretations in order to explore more possibilities is one such strategy. Tightening so as to make better prediction is another. Clients can also choose to modify their constructs. This is especially useful when the implications of conflicting constructs make life uncomfortable for them. They can use their therapists to test their constructs, by validating or invalidating them; and they can try to become more aware of their as yet unarticulated constructs. Sometimes it is only one pole of a construct which is unarticulated, as it is in the negatively polarized views of people who are depressed. Also, when such testing proves difficult to do, they can use help from therapists to recognize their own construct systems, so that superordinate constructs that are no longer appropriate for their lifestyle can become less central and influential.

All of these therapeutic strategies involve some form of reconstruction or reinterpretation. When people become aware that they are responding to their construing of events rather than to the events themselves, they are no longer overwhelmed by their constructs. And when they become aware of their own role in creating those constructs, they can change their construing. Clients can reconstrue any of the events they remember during their lives, but that reconstruing is limited by the permeability of their constructs. Permeability refers to how readily those constructs can be applied to interpret new events and make predictions based on them.

Narrative Reconstruction

Clients come to therapy with many different narratives which they have drawn from their lives. These separate narratives generally fit together to create the sense of continuity apparent in a person's life story and in one's sense of self. This continuity may not be clear to client or therapist initially. The client may offer some clues (descriptions of earlier experiences or problems, beliefs about motives and actions, incidents that are significant), any of which may require the combined attention of the client and the therapist. These clues may suggest clients' dissatisfaction with the self constructed in their stories. Yet attending to their stories acknowledges clients as tellers of their own tales, and so as able to choose to retell them.

Therapists of many theoretical approaches are beginning to advocate the telling and retelling of their clients' stories (Berger, 1989; Mills & Crawley, 1986). It is one thing however to ask clients to tell their stories; it requires of them quite a different skill to retell it. A lot depends on identifying with the client that part of their story that is problematic. The client may identify the problem as something about particular actions or events. But clearly a story is more than its content. It adds an order or sequence to events, as well as context for those events, which become clear as clients are permitted to tell their stories. On the basis of their history, clients expect or anticipate their futures to unfold similarly, to be "the same old story." The therapist's role is not to become the storyteller for clients, but to encourage them to see that a reconstruction of their story is possible.

There is a range of constructivist ways in which clients can retell their stories (Viney & Crooks, 1990). They can be encouraged to test possible courses of action for them, by creating new stories or retelling old ones; and this can be done with their family and friends, with their therapists or in the safety of their own imaginations. Depending on the ways in which their narratives fail to be useful to them, they can be loosened or tightened. They can also be dilated to include a wider range of events or constricted to narrow their focus. Role play can be used for narrative reconstruction. It can also be helpful to explore a range of endings for the story, even by the relatively simple technique of asking clients to imagine such alternative outcomes.

Clients are not always ready for narrative reconstruction. This may be because they do not recognize their own role as storytellers. They are unwilling to accept authorship of their own stories, so they cling to the passive, blameless roles of being the victims in other people's stories. They may feel that they lack the creativity to reconstruct their stories, or that it would be a worthless story even if they tried. Or it may be because of the concrete realist nature of their construing, in which they stolidly maintain a view of events as fixed and inevitable and not interpreted by them in any way. They may believe that everyone's story is prewritten: that the content, the sequence, and the context are rigidly determined. Clients who still have part of their narratives unverbalized have difficulty, as do those whose ability to reinterpret is reduced by strong emotions. It may also be because clients have competing narratives and the chance of reconstruction is incorrectly perceived as forcing them to make a choice between them. These clients need to expand the permeability of their construing, in order to see that there is more than one way to tell their stories.

THE PROMISCUOUS CLIENT

Biographical Details

Paul was 38 years old and had worked successfully in the television industry, earning enough to allow him to maintain his living standards by only occasional part-time work. His family were all living in other states. He was currently in a close relationship with a man somewhat younger than he was, which had lasted for 2 years; but it had had many ups and downs. He had been HIV-infected for some 5 years; but was still asymptomatic. He had developed a promiscuous lifestyle which he described as "life in the fast lane." "I feel as if I *have* to participate. There are the clubs and the dance halls and the pubs and the outings. There are a lot of drugs . . . , a lot of physical abuse." However, he seemed already to be looking for ways out of this lifestyle since he had started working with a psychodrama group and had attended a number of meditation retreats. His original contract with his constructivist therapist was an open-ended, exploratory one. Eventually, they worked together for nine sessions over an 18 week period. Before that reconstructive therapy is described, an account of some of the more central and influential constructs in Paul's system of constructs will be provided, together with the narratives in which he was applying them to maintain his promiscuous life style.

The Client's Major Constructs

Paul applied a number of constructs to make sense of his situation. One crucial bipolar construct was "close to others" versus "socially isolated," and another was "real with other people" versus "wearing a mask." He also saw himself and other people as either "of use to people" or not, as well as "having a grip on themselves" or not. "Healthy" versus "unhealthy" was another key construct, while "losing things" versus "getting rid of things" proved to be another. "Achievement and competition" versus "passivity" dominated his experience too. He also talked of "emotional baggage" which he needed to deal with. Anxiety proved to be one part of this "baggage," since he was dimly aware, and had been for some time, that the range of his construct system was not sufficient to allow him to anticipate some of his own and others' actions effectively. He had been angry for a long time, seeking validation for his constructs about closeness to others in his often frenetic casual sexual encounters and being repeatedly disappointed. He was also experiencing occasional bouts of shame, when he recognized that some of his actions did not fit well with the ways in which he liked to view himself.

The Client's Promiscuity–Promoting Narratives

Paul has four major narratives in which he was using these constructs to maintain his promiscuity. The First was about the pull of competition.

> It is a very strenuous kind of lifestyle but you can't afford to lose a foothold in it. The competition to be in there, to be

> seen, to be in demand is tremendous. And of course this lifestyle is very physical. I mean you can have more than one physical experience a day, sometimes, up to 10 a day. You have to be in it; you have to be seen; you have to participate.

The second indicated his fear of loneliness and abandonment.

> If you don't stick in the fast lane, you become socially isolated. You can become socially unacceptable so easily. Then you become on the outer, and the opportunities of meeting people who are potential partners whether sexual or for friendship, diminishes.

The third narrative further explored this fear.

> When you don't go along with this lifestyle, you lose out on things. You lose too much–enjoyment, but most of all you lose friends.

The fourth, containing the seeds of some of his feelings of shame, he shared with many other members of his close-knit gay community.

> I can only be real when I'm with gay people. It's like I used to go to work with one identity or even a kind of mask. Then I came home and took off the mask and became my real self.

In terms of our criteria for useful narratives, these are integrated, consistent, and time-binding; but the course of action they promote is ultimately self-defeating, as well as dangerous for others, and any power and hope they promise to their narrator is illusory.

NARRATIVE RECONSTRUCTION BY THIS CLIENT

During therapy Paul was able to make good use of the opportunities available to test his construct system. That some of his constructs were quite permeable had already been evidenced in his experimenting with psychodrama and meditation. His major blocks to change were, not a rejection of his roles as construer and story teller, which he accepted readily, but the intense emotions of anxiety, anger and shame which early in therapy threatened to overwhelm him. As he strengthened his meditational techniques they gave him more control over these emotions. In fact his therapist encouraged him to use his concurrent experiments with meditation and psychodrama, together with those they devised together for their relationship and with others, to explore alternative ways of construing his world. He was thus successful in reorganizing his construct system to some extent, reapplying his old constructs and even creating a new construct for his use.

He was initially prompted to risk changing the stories which supported his promiscuous lifestyle by his "healthy" versus "unhealthy" construct. He was concerned that his body could hardly be described as "healthy," and knowledgeable enough about the functioning of the immune system to recognize that, as an HIV-infected man, he needed to be healthy to resist immune function deterioration.

> I need to stop going out so much. I should make sure that I cut down my drug consumption, including tea and coffee. I'm going to cut down on all the drugs which I believe have an effect on the immune system. I will do things in moderation and listen to my body more.

And as this focus on health increased, so his reconstruction of the first of his promiscuity-promoting narratives began.

> One thing my friends say I'm losing is ambition. I don't need to get anywhere; I'm there. I need to make it better rather than accumulate more of it.

Of course this form of reconstruction was much aided by his experiments with meditation.

Paul also began to deal more effectively with his fears of isolation and loss, so central to two of his earlier narratives. Some sense of guilt is apparent in this narrative in which he may not be living up to his own expectations of himself in relation to others if he is "ruthless" about them.

> I'm getting rid of people who are no use to me, who are in fact negative influences on my life. I'm becoming quite ruthless in a way, but in a really healthy way, by recognizing what is, and is not good for me.

His narrative about being real only with gay people was receiving continuing invalidation from his becoming real with his therapist, and also being able to do so with heterosexual people in the psychodrama group. He was able to move toward this reconstructed narrative about an important part of the gay scene.

> I'm making conscious choices to make sure that most of my friends aren't connected to AIDS because I think it's unhealthy to live, breath, eat and sleep with AIDS, which is what I did for a while.

And he moved to this one about the gay sex scene.

> I've gone beyond the stage of wanting to go out to bars and pick up strangers. . . . I don't enjoy that kind of sex any more.

The practice of meditation became more and more important to Paul, and his meditational experiences, together with construing and reconstruing of them by client and therapist in therapy, enabled him to develop a number of new narratives that were of value to him in maintaining his changed lifestyle.

> Meditation has become a big force in my life. It gives me a lot of energy and strength, because it really centers my energy; and I'm learning to live every minute to the fullest. It involves a whole change in mental attitude toward the way you live. It's life-affirming. I'm now choosing life rather than death.

Another of these narratives showed how he had moved from fearing that he would lose objects and people to being much less dependent on them.

> Things that I was quite heavily invested in have lost their attraction . . . like possessions. I have accepted that the time and energy I devoted to some of my possessions was inappropriate. I just don't have the time any more. It's an attitude that understands 'I'm rid of that' rather than 'what am I losing'?

He, who had hidden his HIV antibody positive status from many people for fear of rejection, was able to say, and begin to live by, this narrative:

> I think that it's very important that those of us who have the emotional resources to do so, are very open about being HIV antibody positive, to reduce fear in the community, to be educators, and just to show other people who are HIV-infected that we can be really well and healthy and lead normal lives.

These reconstructed narratives are, like the ones he used earlier, integrated, consistent and time-binding. Yet the courses of action they propose are now helpful to both himself and others; and the power of decision making and the hope of contentment they offer him are far from illusory.

RECONSTRUCTIVE THERAPY AND OTHER THERAPEUTIC APPROACHES

This account of reconstructive therapy with a promiscuous client began with a review of the major concepts of personal construct psychology, to which the concept of narrative has been added. This was followed by a review of personal construct therapy, to which the concept of narrative reconstruction was added. Then the client, Paul, was introduced: his biographic and lifestyle details, the constructs he was using initially to make sense of his world and the narratives he was using to maintain his promiscuous behavior. The therapeutic processes of reconstruing his narratives were described, together with the reconstrued narratives he was able to develop to maintain his now healthier and safer life style.

Readers may be asking, What kind of therapy is this? Is it a cognitive therapy? Is it like those developed by Beck (1976) and Ellis (1988)? Using the analysis of these therapies by Mahoney and his colleagues (Mahoney & Gabriel, 1987; Mahoney & Lyddon, 1988), reconstructive therapy, like those of Beck and Ellis, can be said to be cognitive therapy; but with that the commonalities end. The approaches of Beck and Ellis are rationalist, while this is constructivist. We would therefore like to conclude this paper with the central assumptions on which these approaches differ, the different kinds of concepts they have developed, and the different therapeutic practices that flow from these assumptions and concepts.

While for the rationalist therapist the world is assumed to be singular and stable, for the constructivist it is relative and ever changing. Paul's presentation of the context for his promiscuous behavior, for example, was therefore seen by his therapist as flexible, rather than fixed, as it would have been for a rationalist. Also, for a rationalist therapist, change, including therapeutic change, is assumed to take place through associative learning, while for the constructivist therapist it consists of a refinement of mental representations of events, or, in this version of the therapy, of Paul's narratives about his behavior.

Also, while rationalist therapists conceptualize the central system of our bodies as a center for control, for constructivist therapists it is a center for the promotion of order and organization. Paul's central nervous system was, therefore, invited to order and reorder his ways of making sense of his promiscuity. Reality is also represented differently in the two approaches. For rationalist therapists it is copied or mirrored; for constructivist therapists, it is, of course, constructed or created. There was no question in Paul's therapist's mind, then, about whether his narratives were accurate or not, only about what their implications were for his behavior.

The difference in practice between the two approaches are important too. The interventions of rationalist therapists would have been ahistorical and problem-focused. Paul's reconstructive therapist, however, acknowledged the role of his personal history in the development of his promiscuity-promoting narratives and then focused on the processes of their reconstruction. For rationalist therapists, the client's promiscuity would have been considered to be a dysfunction or deficit which needed to be remedied. Paul's promiscuity, however, was considered by his therapist to arise from discrepancies between his contextual stressors and his capacities to cope with those stressors. Rationalist therapists view other client's blocks to therapeutic movement as showing a lack of motivation, whereas this constructivist therapist viewed Paul's blocks as appropriately self-protective for him. Finally, the therapeutic relationship for rationalist therapists is one of instruction of the client by the therapist; yet Paul's constructivist therapist provided a safe and accepting context for some of his experiments and for discussion of others, that is, for exploration.

This constructivist therapy proved useful in helping to move a promiscuous client out of "the fast lane." It enabled him to use his other methods of exploration, psychodrama and especially mediation, to come to see that his promiscuous life style could lead eventually to even his own death. He was, he finally recognized, on the road to at least two kinds of death: a physical death through his vulnerability to declining immune function and consequent opportunistic infections, and a spiritual and emotional death through his increasing alienation from his own psyche through sexual and drugbased overstimulation. It is well that, at the conclusion of therapy, he could say: "I'm now choosing life rather than death."

REFERENCES

Agar, M. & Hobbs, J.J. (1982). Interpreting discourse: Coherence and analysis of ethnographic interviews. *Discourse Process, 5*, 1-32.

Bannister, D. (1975). Personal construct theory psychotherapy. In D. Bannister (Ed.), *Issues and approaches in the psychological therapies*. London: Wiley.

Beck, A.T. (1976). *Cognitive therapy and the emotional disorders*. New York: Meridian.

Berger, D.W. (1989). Developing the story in psychotherapy. *American Journal of Psychotherapy, 43*, 248-259.

Carr, D. (1985). Life and the narrator's art. In H.J. Silverman & D. Ihde (Eds.), *Hermeneutics and deconstruction*. New York: State University of New York.

Cohler, B.J. (1982). Personal narrative and life course. In P. Baltes & O.G. Brim (Eds.), *Life span development and behaviour*, Vol. 4. New York: Academic Press.

Ellis, A. (1984). The essence of RET–1984. *Journal of Rational Emotive Therapy, 2*, 19-26.

Epting, F.R. (1984). *Personal construct counseling and psychotherapy*. New York: Wiley.

Fransella, F. (1972). *Personal change and reconstruction*. London: Academic Press.

Fransella, F. (1988). Individual psychotherapy. In E. Button (Ed.), *Personal construct theory and mental health*. Beckenham: Croom Helm.

Kelly, G.A. (1955). *The psychology of personal construct*. Vols. 1 & 2. New York: Norton.

Kurtzman, H.S. (1987). Deconstruction and psychology: An introduction. *New Ideas in Psychology, 5*, 33-71.

Labov, W. (1972). The transformation of experience in narrative syntax. In W. Labov (Ed.), *Language in the inner city*. Philadelphia, Pennsylvania: University of Pennsylvania Press.

Landfield, A.W. (1971). *Personal construct systems in psychotherapy*. Chicago: Rand McNally.

Macmillan, A. (1989). Developmental narratives: The construction of life stories in therapy. Conference on Psychology, Psychotherapy and Story Telling, Dumfries, Scotland.

Mahoney, M.J., & Gabriel, T.J. (1987). Psychotherapy and the cognitive sciences: An evolving alliance. *Journal of Cognitive Psychotherapy, 1*, 39-59.

Mahoney, M.J., & Lyddon, W.J. (1988). Recent developments in cognitive approaches to counselling and psychotherapy. *The Counselling Psychologist, 16*, 190-234.

Mair, J.M.M. (1988). Kelly, Bannister and a story-telling psychology. *International Journal of Personal Construct Psychology, 2*, 1-14.

Mair, J.M.M. (1990). Telling psychological tales. *International Journal of Personal Construct Psychology, 3*, 121-136.

Mills, J.C., & Crowley, R.J. (1986). *Therapeutic metaphors for children and the child within*. New York: Brunner/Mazel.

Mishler, E. F. (1986a). *Research interviewing: Context and narrative*. London: Harvard University Press.

Neimeyer, R.A., & G.J. (Eds.) (1987). *Personal construct therapy casebook*. New York: Springer.

Sarbin , T.R. (Ed.) (1986). *Narrative psychology*. New York: Praeger.

Schafer, R. (1980). Narration in the psychoanalytic dialogue. *Critical Inquiry, 7*, 29-53.

Viney, L.L. (1989). Reconstructive psychotherapy. University of Wollongong: Unpublished manuscript.

Viney, L.L. (in press) Psychotherapy as shared reconstruction. *International Journal of Personal Construct Psychology*.

Viney, L.L. (1990). The construing widow: Dislocation and adaptation in bereavement. *The Psychotherapy Patient, 6*(3/4), 207-222.

Viney, L.L., Benjamin, Y.N., & Preston, C. (1988). Promoting independence in the elderly. *Clinical Gerontologist, 24*, 71-82.

Viney, L.L., Benjamin, Y.N., & Preston, C. (in press). Personal construct therapy for the elderly. *International Journal of Psychotherapy.*

Viney, L.L., & Bousfield, L. (1989). Narrative analysis: A technique for psychosocial research in AIDS. University of Wollongong: Unpublished paper.

Viney, L.L., Clarke, A.M., Bunn, T.A., & Benjamin, Y.N. (1985a). The evaluation of three crisis intervention programs for general hospital patients. *British Journal of Medical Psychology, 58*, 75-86.

Viney, L.L., Clarke, A.M., Bunn, T. A., & Benjamin, Y.N. (1985b). Crisis intervention counseling: An evaluation of long and short term effects. *Journal of Counseling Psychology, 32*, 29-39.

Viney, L.L., & Crooks, L. (1990). Retelling narratives about AIDS: Strategies for clients and counselors. University of Wollongong: Unpublished manuscript.

Promiscuity, Psychotherapy, and Strong Laughter

Alvin R. Mahrer
Richard Markow
Patricia A. Gervaize

SUMMARY. From a large data pool of 280 audiotaped psychotherapy sessions, six sessions were identified as containing a series of discrete strong-laughter outbursts. By examining the content of verbal statements in each strong-laughter outburst, and by comparisons with the verbal content of consequent client statements, the balance of client statements in the sessions, and changes that occur sequentially across sessions, the findings indicate that strong-laughter outbursts were uniquely characterized by distinctively high loadings of risky verbal behavior. Implications were drawn regarding the clinical meaning and therapeutic use of strong-laughter outbursts in psychotherapy.

This is not an article about the use of strong laughter in psychotherapy with patients who are promiscuous. Even further, it is a research study, complete with a reasonably rigorous design and statistical analyses. A good case can be made that this article does not belong in a theme volume on the promiscuous patient, but there are two reasons that warrant its inclusion. One is that the impetus for doing the study must be credited to a woman whose profession is prostitution. She was seen in a large clinic whose therapy rooms

---

Al Mahrer, PhD, is in the School of Psychology, University of Ottawa. Richard Markow, PhD, is Clinical Professor in the School of Psychology, University of Ottawa. Patricia A. Gervaize, PhD, is Research Clinical Psychologist, Department of Obstetrics and Gynecology, University of Ottawa School of Medicine.
Address correspondence to Al R. Mahrer, PhD, School of Psychology, University of Ottawa, Ottawa, Canada, K1N 6N5.

were not sufficiently soundproofed to retain repeated outbursts of strong hearty laughter in the initial session conducted by an intern following an experiential psychotherapeutic approach. This prompted some vigorous staff discussions on the appropriateness or inappropriateness of strong laughter in psychotherapy, and this in turn led to the research study. The second reason is that we believe the findings bear directly on how strong laughter may be used by practitioners; and our preference is to bridge the gap between clinical research and practice by reaching the practitioner audience, whether or not the clients may be described as promiscuous.

The target event is laughter that is strong rather than mild, and occurs somewhat infrequently in the session rather than as a frequent stylistic characteristic of the client. A review of the clinical theory and research on strong laughter in psychotherapy (Mahrer & Gervaize, 1984) indicated that this event is expressly welcomed in humanistic-experiential approaches (e.g., Bugental, 1976; Farrelly & Brandsma, 1974; Greenwald, 1975; Harman, 1981; Jackins, 1965; Mahrer, 1989; Mindess, 1971; Perls, 1970; Polster & Polster, 1973) and is regarded as a pathological indicator in psychoanalytic-psychodynamic approaches (e.g. Bergler, 1976; Freud, 1905/1960; Koestler, 1964; Kubie, 1971; Levine, 1976; Plessner, 1970; Zuk, 1966).

Accordingly, it is understandable that the four studies of the therapeutic usefulness of strong laughter have been within humanistic-experiential approaches. Two studies (Nichols, 1974; Nichols & Bierenbaum, 1978) reported positive relations between psychotherapeutic outcome and strong laughter. A third study identified therapist methods and procedures antecedent to the occurrence of strong laughter (Gervaize, Mahrer, & Markow, 1985). The fourth study examined the statements containing strong laughter in a large number of clients, and reported a high incidence (94.3%) of content judged as risky (outrageous, impulsive, shocking, tabooed, dangerous, exciting, absurd, outlandish) (Mahrer, Markow, Gervaize, & Boulet, 1987).

The purpose of the present study was to learn more about the psychotherapeutic usefulness of strong laughter outbursts by examining each sequential instance across individual sessions. What are the relatively immediate consequences of strong laughter? Do these consequences cumulate across a session? What may be learned about the nature and degree of verbal behavior in strong-laughter statements as compared with statements in the balance of the session? The findings allow us to identify such strong-laughter outbursts as a unique psychotherapeutic event, to frame some inferences about the clinical meaning and significance of strong laughter, and to suggest ways in which strong laughter be used to facilitate the psychotherapeutic process.

METHODOLOGY

Strong-Laughter Sessions

Selection of the session began with a data pool of 280 audiotaped therapy sessions with 58 individual adult clients and with 24 therapists representative of a broad range of approaches. From this pool, all instances of strong laughter were identified by a method used by Nichols (1974); Nichols and Bierenbaum (1978); and Gervaize, Mahrer, and Markow (1985). A doctoral student in clinical psychology listened to all 280 sessions and identified each instance of strong laughter in statements containing at least four words, together with an equal number of instances of mild-moderate laughters. Independent ratings by two subsequent judges yielded a confirmed subpool of strong-laughter statements. All sessions were thereby identified that contained at least three strong laughters as discrete events, or as occurring in at least three sets of consequent client statements, each separated by intervening non-laughter client statements. In order to eliminate strong laughter as a frequent stylistic characteristic of clients, sessions were deleted that contained 12 or more strong laughters occurring as discrete events or 12 or more sets of consequent client strong-laughter statements.

This procedure yielded six sessions conducted by three therapists with six clients. Three of the clients were female, and three were male. All the sessions were from the mid-phases of therapy; and dealt with a range of topics and problems including marital and family relationships, bodily phenomena and complaints, heterosexual relationships, and feeling-states such as aggression, worthlessness, and dependency. The three therapists identified themselves as representing humanistic-experiential approaches. Two sessions contained three discrete strong laughters or sets of consequent strong laughters, three sessions contained four, and one session contained nine discrete strong laughters or sets of consequent strong laughters. In each of the six sessions, the strong laughters were evenly distributed across the session rather than unevenly occurring in any of the thirds of the session.

Category System of Strong-Laughter Statements

The verbal content of statements containing strong laughter was categorized using a system derived from a review of strong laughter in psychotherapy (Mahrer & Gervaize, 1984) and refined in subsequent studies (Gervaize, Mahrer, & Markow, 1985; Mahrer, Markow, Gervaize, & Boulet, 1987). Briefly summarized, the system is as follows:

1. *Expressed risky behavior.* The client is expressing (doing, carrying out, engaging in) behavior that is risky (outrageous, impulsive, shocking, tabooed, devilish, wicked, bad, explosive, threatening, dangerously exciting, absurd, outlandish).
   - 1.1 *Toward the therapist.* The client is expressing risky behavior directly toward the therapist as the object or target or recipient of the behavior.
   - 1.2 *Toward other figure.* The client is expressing risky behavior directly toward some other figure as the object or target or recipient of the behavior. The other figure is present in fantasy, memory, or imagination.
   - 1.3 *About oneself.* The client is talking about (admitting, revealing, criticizing) something about herself or himself. The risky behavior is that of talking about that particular aspect or element of oneself.
2. *Described risky behavior.* The client is describing (reporting, relating, recounting) a risky behavior that may be carried out by the client or by some other person.

3. *Reacted-to risky behavior.* The client is reacting to a risky behavior that was expressed or described by the therapist or client. The feelinged reaction may be positive or negative.
4. *Pathological state.* The client's behavior is indicative of psychopathology (serious problems, emotional illness, psychotic process, disturbance, inner chaos, inability to cope, psychic threat). The state may be shown directly, or alluded to or signified. This category is exclusive of categories 1-3.
5. *Other.* The client is not expressing, describing, or reacting to risky behavior; nor is the client's statement indicative of psychopathology. This is the "all other" category.

Judges

The four judges included two clinical psychologists and two advanced doctoral students in clinical psychology. All judges had a minimum of 3 years experience using category systems for judging client statements from audiotapes and transcripts, including a minimum of 35 hours of experience using the present system.

Procedure

Each judge was given a training manual including a fuller description of the seven categories and clinical examples of each. Because each judge was familiar with the category system, no additional training was required.

The six sessions comprised a total of 813 therapist statements and 813 client statements, with client statement defined as all the words spoken by the client, preceded and followed by words spoken by the therapist. The audiotapes and transcripts were segmented in 32 blocks, each containing approximately 30 sequential therapist and client statements. These 32 blocks were presented in random order to three of the judges who independently rated each client statement using the seven-fold category system. If all three judges agreed, the client statement was included in the data analysis. If no pair of judges agreed, the statement was deleted from further study. If only two of the three judges agreed, the fourth judge rated the client statement, and the statement was included in the data analysis provided that the fourth judge confirmed the rating.

RESULTS AND DISCUSSION

Of the total of 813 client statements, only 4 failed to achieve agreement among at least two of the three judges, and these were deleted from further study. However, 27 of the 813 client statements achieved only 67% agreement among the three judges. Of these 27, 17 achieved concurrence from the fourth judge, and the remaining 10 were deleted from further study. Accordingly, the data consisted of 799 (98.3%) of the original 813 client statements. Of the 799 client statements, 647 (80.9%) were judged as falling in the "other" category, 13 (1.6%) were judged as indicating a pathological state, and the balance of 139 (17.4%) were judged as containing risky verbal behavior.

Strong-Laughter Statements as Uniquely Characterized by Risky Verbal Behaviors

We were interested in the extent to which strong-laughter statements were uniquely characterized by risky verbal behaviors as compared with the balance of client statements in the sessions. In order to effect a more stringent comparison, the five client statements immediately consequent to strong laughters were excluded from analysis.

The results are given in Table 1. In the six sessions, there were 47 strong-laughter statements, of which 45 (95.7%) contained risky verbal behavior. In contrast, of the 617 other client statements, only 70 (11.3%) contained risky verbal behavior. The heavy predominance of risky verbal behaviors in strong-laughter statements as compared with other client statements were 100.0% and 12.6%, 100.0% and 9.2%, 100.0% and 23.4%, 100.0% and 2.0%, 83.3% and 16.8%, and 83.3% and 2.2% in sessions 1-6 respectively.

These findings appear to indicate that in therapies that value the occurrence of strong laughter, these strong-laughter statements seem to be singularly characterized by risky verbal behaviors as compared with the balance of client statements in the session. It may well be that part of the therapeutic value of strong laughter lies in the saturation of risky verbal behaviors, and that there is some justification for using therapeutic methods explicitly useful in pro-

Sessions	Strong Laughter Statements N	Strong Laughter Statements Risky Behavior Statements	Other Statements N	Other Statements Risky Behavior Statements
1	3	3	87	11
2	8	8	108	10
3	12	12	77	18
4	12	12	51	1
5	6	5	161	27
6	6	5	133	3
Total	47	45	617	70

Table 1: Distribution of Risky Behavior Statements in Strong Laughter and Other Statements in Sessions With Six Clients.

moting this risky aspect of strong laughter (Gervaize, Mahrer, & Markow, 1985; Mahrer & Gervaize, 1984).

Categories of Risky Verbal Behaviors Characteristic of Strong Laughter-Statements

The category system enables a closer examination of the categories of risky verbal behaviors that may be characteristic of strong-laughter statements. Using the five categories of risky verbal behavior, comparisons may be made between the distribution of the 45 risky verbal behaviors in the strong-laughter statements and the distribution of the 70 risky verbal behaviors in the balance of the client statements. Again, for purposes of stringency, the five client statements immediately consequent to each strong-laughter statement were deleted from data analysis.

The results are given in Table 2. There were no significant differences in the proportions of risky verbal behavior expressed toward the therapist or expressed toward some other figure. Strong-laughter statements contained a significantly lower proportion of risky verbal behavior expressed about oneself. However, it is interesting that the significant predominance of risky verbal behavior in strong-laughter statements consisted of risky behavior that is reacted-to (33.3%), and that is described (26.6%); and that strong-laughter statements contained a significantly higher proportion of these categories of risky verbal behavior than occurred in the balance of the client statements.

It appears that strong-laughter statements are uniquely characterized by risky verbal behaviors that are described and that are reacted-to, rather than risky verbal behaviors that are expressed toward the therapist, toward some other figure, and especially toward oneself. In terms of the clinical significance of strong laughter, we are inclined to hypothesize that the strong laughter distinctively occurs

Categories of Risky Behavior	Risky Behavior In Strong Laughter N = 45	Risky Behavior In Other Statements N = 70
Expressed Risky Behavior		
Toward Therapist	8.9	12.8
Toward Other Figures	17.8	10.0
About Oneself	13.4	64.4*
Described Risky Behavior	26.6*	10.0
Reacted-To Risky Behavior	23.3*	2.8
Column Total %	100.0	100.0

*$p < .001$

Table 2. Distribution of Categories of Risky Behavior in Strong Laughter and Other Statements in Sessions With Six Clients.

in statements in which the client does not express risky verbal behavior, does not act it out or show risky behavior directly; but rather where the risky behavior is described (related, recounted, reported) by therapist or client, or where a risky behavior was earlier expressed or described by therapist or by client. In short, strong laughter seems to be distinctive as a response to risky behavior rather than as a component of risky behavior that is being directly expressed. It would also appear that what therapists do with the strong laughter would in part be determined by whether the concomitant verbal behavior is directly expressive of risky behavior, or whether the risky behavior is only described or reacted-to.

Risky Behaviors Consequent to Strong Laughter

If the heavy predominance of strong-laughter statements contains risky behavior (95.7%), is the risky behavior limited to the strong-laughter statement or does it carry over to consequent client statements? Clinical and statistical considerations led us to examine the five client statements consequent to the strong laughter, and to compare the proportion of risky behaviors occurring in these sets of consequent statements with the proportion of risky behavior occurring in the balance of the sessions.

The results are given in Table 3. The six sessions included 27 sets of five client statements consequent to the strong-laughter statement. When these data are pooled, the mean percentage of risky behavior in the total of the five statements consequent to strong laughters is 17.7%, insignificantly greater than the mean percentage of risky behavior in the balance of the statements in the sessions (11.7%). Furthermore, this finding is consistent across each of the six sessions wherein there were no significant differences between proportions of risky behaviors in the sets of client statements consequent to the strong laughter as compared with the proportion in the balance of the session.

These findings further confirm the uniqueness of strong-laughter statements. Whereas strong-laughter statements contain a very high percentage of risky behavior (95.7%), this percentage drops precipitously in the immediately consequent five statements (17.7%), and remains at this level in the balance of the statements in the session (11.7%). It appears that the heavy infusion of risky behavior in the

Session	Sets of Client Statements Consequent to Strong Laughter N	Percent Risky Behaviors in Consequent Statements	Percent Risky Behavior in Other Statements
1	3	40.0	12.6
2	4	20.0	9.2
3	3	33.3	23.4
4	9	6.7	2.0
5	4	15.0	16.8
6	4	15.0	2.2

Table 3. Distribution of Risky Behavior Consequent to Strong Laughter and in Other Statements in Sessions With Six Clients.

strong-laughter statements is confined to these statements. Therapists who would be inclined to sustain the risky behaviors following strong-laughter statements are challenged to devise appropriate methods.

The Absence of Cumulative Effects of Strong Laughter

Within individual sessions, is there any evidence of a cumulative effect of strong laughter on immediately consequent client statements? If we examine the proportion of risky behaviors in the five client statements consequent to each strong-laughter outburst, would there be significant increases across the session? As indicated in Table 3, there were three sets of consequent statements in sessions 1 and 3; four in sessions 2, 5, and 6; and nine in session 4.

The results are given in Table 4. Overall, in none of the six sessions was there a sequential increase in the proportions of risky behaviors in the five client statements consequent to strong laugh-

Sequential Set of Client Statements Consequent to Strong Laughter

Session	1	2	3	4	5-9
1	40	40	40		
2	0	0	100	0	
3	100	0	0		
4	0	0	0	0	12
5	0	0	0	0	12
6	40	0	20	0	
Mean	40	6.7	26.7	0	12

Table 4: Percentages of Risky Behavior in Sequential Sets of Client Statements Consequent to Strong Laughter in Sessions With Six Clients.

ter. In each of the six sessions, the proportion of risky behaviors remained constant or reduced over the course of the session. If the data are pooled, the mean proportions of risky behavior in the client statements consequent to the sequential four strong laughters were 40.0, 6.7, 26.7, and 0.0 respectively; and 12.0 in the final five strong-laughter epochs of session 4.

The absence of cumulative effects may be taken as another indication of the uniqueness of strong-laughter statements. If strong laughter is uniquely characterized by risky behavior, especially risky behavior that is described or reacted-to, repeated occurrences of the strong laughter show no evidence of cumulative sequential increases in risky behavior in the consequent client statements.

CONCLUSIONS

The general conclusion is that in sessions conducted by therapists who welcome the discrete, low-frequency occurrence of strong laughter, the strong-laughter outbursts appear to be unique in their high loading of verbal behavior that is risky (outrageous, impulsive, shocking, tabooed, devilish, wicked, bad, explosive, dangerous, exciting, absurd, outlandish). More specifically, the findings may be interpreted as cordial to the following conclusions about the unique characteristics of strong laughter:

1. Strong-laughter statements appear to be unique in that 95.7% of these statements contained risky verbal behaviors, while only 11.3% of the balance of the client statements contained risky verbal behaviors. We are inclined to speculate that strong laughter is an effective and efficient vehicle for the occurrence of risky behavior, that part of the therapeutic value of strong laughter lies in the occurrence of risky behavior, and that there is justification for therapeutic methods explicitly effective in promoting strong laughter that contains risky behavior.

2. As compared with other client statements, strong laughter appears to be unique in containing a significantly larger proportion of risky behavior that is described or reacted-to by the client, but is not unique with regard to risky behavior that is directly expressed. We are inclined to hypothesize that strong laughter is distinctive as a responsive reaction to risky behavior rather than as a component of risky behavior that is directly and immediately expressed. It would appear that what therapists do with the strong laughter may in part be determined by whether the concomitant verbal behavior is directly expressive of risky behavior, or whether the risky behavior is described or reacted-to.

3. Strong-laughter statements are unique in that there were no consequent effects of the high proportion (95.7%) of risky behaviors. In the five client statements consequent to the strong laughter, the proportion of risky behavior dropped precipitously to 17.7%, insignificantly different from the proportion of risky behavior in the balance of the session (11.7%). For therapists who value the occurrence of risky behaviors in strong-laughter statements, methods are called for to sustain the discrete occurrence of the risky verbal behavior.

4. Strong-laughter statements are unique in that there were no cumulative effects of the risky behavior across the session, that is, the proportion of risky behaviors in client statements consequent to

the strong-laughter statement did not indicate cumulative sequential increases.

5. For psychotherapists whose theory of practice values the expression and therapeutic use of behavior that is risky, we suggest (a) the use of methods explicitly designed to promote such strong laughter in conjunction with risky behavior that is expressed, described, or reacted-to by the client; (b) that therapy focus on the risky behavioral component of the strong laughter, especially whether the risky behavior is directly expressed, or merely described or reacted-to; and (c) that therapists use methods to sustain and develop the therapeutic advantage presented in the form of the risky behavior concomitant with the strong laughter.

In other words, when the patient has a strong, hearty laughter, the therapist is presented with something unique. This kind of laughter likely contains a high loading of "risky" behavior that is present, not openly expressed, but is indicated, pointed at, reacted to. Furthermore, this high loading of implied and unexpressed risky behavior is present in the moment of the strong, hearty laughter. It does not persist or cumulate. For therapists who are so inclined, what is important is to use this revealed load of risky behavior. Here is something unique that accompanies the strong-laughter outburst, and for this we thank the promiscuous patient whose hearty laughter opened the way for this clinical research.

REFERENCES

Bergler, E. (1976). *Laughter and the sense of humor.* New York: International Medical Book Corporation.

Bugental, J.F.T. (1970). *The search for existential identity.* San Francisco: Jossey-Bass.

Farrelly, F., & Brandsma, J. (1974). *Provocative therapy.* Fort Collins, CO: Shields.

Freud, S. (1960). *Jokes and their relation to the unconscious.* New York: W.W. Norton. (Original work published 1905)

Gervaize, P.A., Mahrer, A.R., & Markow, R. (1985). Therapeutic laughter: What therapists do to promote strong laughter in patients. *Psychotherapy in Private Practice, 3,* 65-74.

Greenwald, H. (1975). Humor in psychotherapy. *Journal of Contemporary Psychotherapy, 7,* 113-116.

Harman, R.L. (1981). Humor and Gestalt therapy. *VOICES: The Art and Science of Psychotherapy, 16*(4), 62-64.

Jackins, H. (1965). *The human side of human beings: The theory of re-evaluation counselling*. Seattle: Rational Island Publishers.

Koestler, A. (1964). *The act of reaction*. New York: Pantheon.

Kubie, L.S. (1971). The destructive potential of humor in psychotherapy. *American Journal of Psychiatry, 127*, 861-866.

Levine, J. (1976). Humor as a form of therapy: Introduction to a symposium. In A.J. Chapman and H.C. Foot (Eds.). Humor and laughter: *Theory, research, and applications* (pp. 123-125). London: John Wiley.

Mahrer, A.R. (1989). *How to do experiential psychotherapy: A manual for practitioners*. Ottawa: University of Ottawa Press.

Mahrer, A.R., & Gervaize, P.A. (1984). An integrative review of strong laughter in psychotherapy: What it is and how it works. *Psychotherapy, 21*, 510-516.

Mahrer, A.R., Markow, R., Gervaize, P.A., & Boulet, D.B. (1987). Strong laughter in psychotherapy: Concomitant patient verbal behavior and implications for therapeutic use. *VOICES: The Art and Science of Psychotherapy, 23*(1), 80-88.

Mindess, H. (1976). The use and abuse of humor in psychotherapy. In A.J. Chapman and H.C. Foot (Eds.). *Humor and laughter: Theory, research, and applications* (pp. 180-197). London: John Wiley.

Nichols, M.P. (1974). Outcome of brief cathartic psychotherapy. *Journal of Consulting and Clinical Psychology, 42*, 403-410.

Nichols, M.P., & Bierenbaum, H. (1979). Success of cathartic therapy as a function of patient variables. *Journal of Clinical Psychology, 34*, 726-728.

Perls, F. (1970). Four lectures. In J. Fagan and I.L. Shepherd (Eds.). *Gestalt therapy now* (pp. 130-149). Palo Alto, CA: Science and Behavior Books.

Plessner, H. (1970). *Laughing and crying: A study of the limits of human behavior* (3rd ed.). Evanston, IL.: Northwestern University Press.

Polster, E., & Polster, M. (1973). *Gestalt therapy integrated: Contours of theory and practice*. New York: Brunner/Mazel.

Zuk, G.H. (1966). On the theory and pathology and laughter in psychotherapy. *Psychotherapy: Theory, Research and Practice, 3*, 97-101.

The Promiscuity of Psychotherapy

E. Mark Stern

SUMMARY. Psychotherapy involves an uncommon "promiscuity"–a non-exclusive agapeic love. This essay underlines the reasoning behind this vantage point.

Even though you tie a hundred knots–the string remains.
–Sufi Saying

PSYCHOTHERAPY'S PURPOSE

Psychotherapy requires a unique engagement, committing both patient and therapist to a diversified revaluation of memories and personal legends. In its most creative moments, psychotherapy fosters an unmatched reverence for the patient's experience. What constitutes this practice has changed in the course of social, political, and economic events hailing significant shifts in self-construct and the consequent usages of the therapeutic. Yet even in the face of intrusions into psychotherapy practice by third-party payers and the increasing popularity of procedure-oriented managed-care programs, the character of the context of the therapist/patient relationship remains true to the reverence of personal experience.

E. Mark Stern, EdD, Columbia University, 1955, Diplomate in Clinical Psychology of the American Board of Professional Psychology, Fellow of the American Psychological Association, is Professor, Graduate Division of Pastoral and Family Counseling, Iona College, New Rochelle, NY, and is in private practice in New York City and Clinton Corners, NY.

Mailing address: 215 E. 11 St., New York, NY 10003.

PERSONAL AND INTERPERSONAL ASPECTS OF THERAPEUTIC DISCOURSES

Therapeutic discourses emerge as personal chronicles unfold. Reparative processes in psychotherapy crystallize emotional awakenings. While each discourse is distinct and uniquely suited to the respective patient, all may be said to be dedicated to the pursuit of common human goals (Angyal, 1965). Likewise, each discourse qualitatively affects, even as it is radically affected by, the broad range of the therapist's text with other patients.

Collective Interplay

Psychotherapy is the professional practice of broad emotional access and non-exclusive caring. Thus all psychotherapeutic practice is influenced by the collective interplay of psyches. This multiplication of experiences is in some ways parallel to commonplace promiscuity, while for the therapist-patient relationship, exclusive even in its nonexclusivity.

A therapist's professional commitment, though seemingly disjoined by its ambiguous appointment schedule, necessarily invokes an assemblage of variegated patient experiences. Such memories and lingering images act as essential background and contrast for a creative psychotherapy practice, since they help insure it against stagnation. These memories and images are also characteristic of "promiscuity," or otherwise expressed, as unity arising out of diversity. Recalling the words of the ancient philosopher Plotinus (1956):

> It is inevitably necessary to think of all as contained within one nature. . . . But within the unity, the several entities each have (their) own distinct existence. . . . When it takes lot with multiplicity, Being becomes Number by the fact of awakening to manifoldness. (p. 35)

The richer the array of patient experiences, the more resplendent the therapeutic focus. With enlarged vision, each patient of a particular therapist reaches a certain correspondence with the multitude of all other patients who have or have had a place in that therapist's particular practice. As Anna Freud (1980) so wisely observed:

> Patients . . . of one and the same (therapist) behave in the transference as if they were real siblings. . . . (They) compare themselves with each other; they compete; they envy each other in view of alleged parental preferences. Sometimes they may even "combine forces . . . to fight the parent." (p. 418)

What happens in any one therapeutic practice, by necessity, becomes prototypic for all others in that practice. The essence of any single life tends to replicate the essence of the whole. As a consequence of such multiplicity, each of the many selves, in playing out their contrasting and uniquely variegated natures, becomes its own unifying theme.

A Single Core

A therapeutic practice is, more or less, a continuity divisible into separate living histories. For the therapist, this continuity, based on background and contrast, is ultimately bound into an unrivaled context. Contrasting contexts tend to enrich and consolidate the therapist's vision. True to this orientation, each contrasting history finally blends into kindredhood. Kindredhood creates a particular relational ethos of any given psychotherapeutic practice. This conspicuous array of conflicts and confluences forms the basis for the art of differentiating larger contexts, as they progressively relate to each of any one therapist's patients. So it is that each patient, past and present, occupies unique space within the larger context of a therapy practice.

Let us then assume that each patient is related to all others, much in the way that individual notes are germane to a sonorous chord. Counterposing personalities within any one practice ultimately participate in that therapist's necessary intersubjective creativity.

The Discrete and the Continuous

A psychotherapy practice is a spontaneously developing text. Precisely because of its capacity to be in tune with many disparate personalities, the art of psychotherapy deals with both the discrete and the continuous. Thus in any given practice, the patient can be recognized by his or her unique interaction with the larger field. This constantly expanding texture embodies encounters ranging from the superficial or undeveloped to those in which a climate of trust and intimacy has been forged.

Each aspect of the texture becomes even more luminous in the ongoing course of a therapeutic practice. Gradually, what was formerly seen as the dispassionate and/or unconnected, evolves into the larger texture of the therapist becoming an intimate to the many. This intimacy is ultimately a shared wealth since each encounter in any one practice affects all others in that practice. Furthermore, as this commonwealth of intimacy touches all, it, by necessity, transforms all. In any one practice, caring and intimacy become more grounded and profound as they are rediscovered again and again with and within each new encounter. It is in the collective of these encounters that psychotherapies are born. While no two patients may require the same technical approach, each road taken with any one patient stamps its imprint on subsequent episodes with others. In a similar vein: As the therapist reckons with what had been employed with past patients, this reckoning too becomes subject to change given the therapists' subsequent experiences. I well recall seeing a patient I had not seen for several years. She was once again in the throes of an obsessive-compulsive attack. My newer work with her had challenged her considerably and with rapid success. The patient reported that her visits with me, dating back 5 years, were only now making a new kind of sense. She suggested that we meet every year or so in order that we might recapitulate the earlier therapy.

A PROMISCUITY OF PSYCHOTHERAPY PRACTICE

Psychotherapy is promiscuous to its core. Yet, definitions fail and fail again. Here it is noted as the broad-based format underlying non-exclusive caring within a professional context. Noting the extent of lives the therapist must be responsive to, is it not fair to say that the best of therapy empathically strategizes at recycling the personal, making it more available in the life span of a given practice. The horde of its atonal transvaluations ferments its promiscuous nature, thus allowing for a communication process, no less personal for its willingness to engage the broadest array of seekers. For the therapist, being therapeutic is tantamount to being in ways both known and unknown *as-the-others*. This common core of therapy, finding its center in the practitioner, becomes even more personalized as the psychotherapy endeavor expands.

Therapist as Non-Exclusive "Lover"

The therapeutic discourse elicits a subtle awareness that the patient is not isolated from those in the therapist's history. Regardless of the way isolation may have been experienced, therapy offers the urge to become a part of a larger life (Angyal, 1965). Elemental to this notion is the premise that the practicing psychotherapist tends to a larger Gestalt, a tending that calls forth the overdeveloping presence of a preeminent superindividuality. Given that this superindividual fact of life owes its existence to the interplay of patients, both past and present, each serves as a co-determinant. Each has its unique position in the therapist's life. The therapist's fulfillment ranges around the tendency to give order to the course of professional life and to ultimately reckon with this course's coherence and unity, nourished by disparate and unique clinical experiences.

Each patient, searching for inner integration, is at the same time a co-carrier of the superindividuality "in a similar way that the cells of an organism are not only the loci of a cell life but participants and carriers of the life of the total organism (Angyal, 1941, p. 168.) This witnessing of a trend toward superindividuality is akin to a ministerial vocation (Stern, 1973).

Like other sacred callings, the work of the therapist involves the capacity to make both universal and particular sense out of many experiential worlds. The dedicated therapist's own vision can never be absent in this pursuit. By vocation this psychotherapist is the non-exclusive "lover" of a vast variety of others. Patients and therapist, those loved and their lover, correspond to the other's extended experience. This seamless nexus defines the staggering potentials alive in the polymorphic nature of a given psychotherapy practice.

The therapist's obligation to prepare for the widest variety of clientele helps expand his or her personal perspective. This therapeutic promiscuousness underscores the fundamental premise that both therapist and patient, while simultaneously autonomous, are regularly afforded the opportunity to engage in a constantly changing, welcoming context. Contexts arising out of a promiscuous process permeate and challenge the arbitrary boundaries which separate past, present, and future; revises the internal conflicts between the imaginal and the objective; and revivifies concerns common to self and others. Each context, though related to all others, must be guaranteed exclusivity and personal reverence. Each patient is entitled to express a unique presence within the therapist's agenda.

Transference and Countertransference Issues

The keynote of the therapist's training is the promiscuity of his or her ongoing practice. This training is itself a therapy which both engages and draws upon an extensive assortment of experiences with past and present patients. If there be cautions and risks appendant to this promiscuity, even they tend to counter a form of therapeutic detachment which keeps many therapists at an aseptic distance from their patients (Bugenthal, 1987). Without risking caring concern, all tides could well turn into a deadening vacuum.

Though in a newer key, both transference and countertransference play an active role in the promiscuous process. Transference translated from the Latin suggests a certain bearing across the lines. Psychotherapy invokes webs of interlacing lines, not only resonating from the patient's earliest relationships, but also reflecting the vast context within the therapist's practice. The latter transference is often stimulated by the therapist's day- in and day-out subjective experiences with other patients. Transference arising out of the context of the therapist's practice cannot always be "interpreted." The therapist cannot refer to concrete others, except as part of a group therapy experience. More than not, the therapist notes signs of serendipity. He or she may note ways in which a particular feeling tone has happened in a like manner at another juncture of practice, either earlier in the space of the day or week, or perhaps many years before. In these instances, his or her best course of action might be simply to take reverential note of the "repetition" and allow its presence to make greater use of the new opportunity which arises out of an earlier instance. After searching the patient's impression of how a reaction or response may be related to persons very much in the patient's own history, I have been known to comment on the mood or ambiance the patient may be sensitive to in the therapeutic setting.

Eyeing a horizontal transference, I once made a remark to a woman who frequently expressed her discomfort at sitting on the "warm spot" of my leather couch. Incidentally, the person who had preceded her in the office had been sitting elsewhere, so that the spot could not have logically undergone any temperature changes. "It appears," I said, "that you are sensitive to another person's presence. (Pause) One who was either 'too hot' for you or just may have brought you some needed warmth." This patient, forever vigilant when it came to her personal boundaries, followed the rest of the session expressing strong feelings about her unrelenting loneliness. "And the warmth in the sofa?" I queried. "Yes," she replied, "when I come here I seem to get close to what it is I really yearn for." I spent several final minutes of that session asking her to muse on the warmth of the seat as some partial clue to allowing for an approach to where her yearnings were leading her.

Reverential Promiscuity

The promiscuous therapist continues a central dialogue with several patients in any one day. The matrix of such therapy practice is always in process. An expansive, albeit promiscuous psychotherapy, absolves its participants from clinging to fixed patterns. The principals known as "me" and "you" begin to re-cognize each other, synchronistically unifying within an array of archetypal possibilities–each transcending a single identity.

A woman who had been struggling with fertility problems caught sight of a recent patient who sat in the waiting room with her newborn. "Good things are happening here," she said. "If I don't conceive a baby soon, I do sense that you know what I'm missing. Moreover, people with babies are not problem free. But just seeing that woman holding her baby made me think of what I could bring here." The next session she had remembered that I'd asked to see some snapshots of her early life "Here they are. I feel as if I'm just now bringing my long ignored 'kid' into this room."

A promiscuous psychotherapy practice includes the widest variety of experience carried, consciously or unconsciously, to each participant. Each respective offering is valued for its unique source, even as each becomes essential to the therapist's shared discourse.

Again, the promiscuous therapist faithfully courts each patient as a singular expression of the greater whole. This attitude gives due reverence to the communality of reveries, fantasies, dreams, ambitions, disappointments, reflections, and imaginings. Within this reverential practice any one patient, without any conscious intent, is seen as deeply affecting others. It may come as little surprise to the seasoned therapist to recollect how two or more patients may present a similar dream. And it may come as no further surprise to note how the therapist's sensitivity in dealing with one of the dreams bears fruit with the others.

Dionysian Aspects

Promiscuous psychotherapy can often be seen as a polymorphous Dionysian enterprise. The therapist is the magus who wears many masks at once. The multifaced therapeutic involvement expands the parameters of psychotherapy. Being with so many may, at times, become a threat to the therapist's identity. Cautions psychotherapist Anthony Storr (1980):

> When psychotherapy is practiced every day and all day, there is a danger of the therapist becoming a non-person; a prostitute parent whose children are not only all illegitimate, but more imaginary than real. (p. 182)

Storr's words are well taken. Yet the practicing therapist must, despite all, remain as fluid and receptive as Dionysus. This Dionysian imperative requires the therapist to ceaselessly pay attention to a labyrinthine unfoldment of lore, legend and humanity. In order to achieve the true meaning of this spirit, the promiscuous therapist must be able to remain attentively immersed in the whole of the discourse.

The Dionysian aspect of therapy rests with the therapist as lover, but certainly *not* as Storr has suggested, as "prostitute." Promiscuity, as used here, confronts and engages the free range of contrasting contexts. These contrasts allow all patients to become courtiers of the therapist, each one eventually embraced by aspects of the Apollonian contrast or by what Joseph Zinker (1977) has viewed as "agapeic" love:

> More a feeling of good will toward humanity than romantic or possessive. . . . It is this love in all its forms which lubricates the creative process between patient and therapist. (p. 6)

The agapeic way of being with each patient requires its own stride. Some therapists have found that on any particular working day, or within a period of a newly discovered therapeutic approach, that a single commentary or interpretation works with many, if not all patients. Each patient, in his or her own way, becomes the inheritor of that day's wisdom.

The agapeic is both Dionysian and Apollonian. These influences form the heartland of any dedicated promiscuous therapy practice. What remains Dionysian is the ecstatic, almost magical flavor. And since promiscuity implies an expansive repertoire, the crystallization of this magic must differ with each practice. Psychotherapy, though rooted in a keen respect for individual differences, becomes all the more enriching, due in no small way to its complexity of the magical collaboration of psyches. Martin Buber has written:

> When a man is singing and cannot lift his voice, and another comes and sings with him, another who can lift his voice, the first will be able to lift his voice too. That is the secret of the bond between spirits. (Zinker, p. 8)

CONCLUSION: THE THERAPIST'S BROAD REPERTOIRE

Much as an orchestral maestro, the therapist too develops as his or her enhanced repertoire emerges. What could well evolve as the core composition of a practice deepens as the therapist caters to each section and to the specific soundings within respective sections. "Psychological induction," reports Jung (1968), "inevitably causes the two parties to get involved in the transformation of the third and to be themselves transformed in the process, and all the time, the doctor's knowledge, like a flickering lamp, is the one dim light in the darkness" (p. 199). It is in these glowing flickers that the blend of Dionysian and Apollonian challenges reaches one and all, severally and individually. And as with all disparate elements in networks which meet and communicate through a dynamic maestro, new awakenings, potentials, and creative obligations are granted their beginnings.

REFERENCES

Angyal, A. (1941). *Foundations for a science of personality.* New York: The Commonwealth Fund.

Angyal, A. (1965). *Neurosis and treatment: A holistic theory.* New York: John Wiley.

Bugenthal, J. (1987). *The art of the psychotherapist.* New York: W.W. Norton.

Freud, A. (1980). *The writings of Anna Freud. Vol. IV.* New York: International Universities Press.

Jung, C. (1968). The psychology of the transference. *Collected works,* (Vol. 16, pp. 163-323). Princeton, NJ: Princeton University Press.

Plotinus (1956). *The enneads.* London: Faber and Faber.

Stern, E. M. (1973)., The psychotherapist as priest. In R. Cox (Ed.) *Religious systems and psychotherapy* (pp. 452-457). Springfield, IL: Charles C Thomas.

Storr, A. (1980). *The art of psychotherapy.* New York: Methuen.

Zinker, J. (1977). *Creative process in Gestalt therapy.* New York: Brunner/Mazel.